LIGHTNING

Lightning Strikes Twice

A true story of one family's triumph over loss

Clive Okill

Hodder & Stoughton
LONDON SYDNEY AUCKLAND

This is a true story. In some cases names and places
have been changed or omitted altogether to protect
confidences shared and to avoid any embarrassment, but
the names of the members of my family are as stated.

Permission has kindly been given by Word Books to extract
the poem 'Children Learn What They Live' by Dorothy Law
Nolte from *How To Be A Hero To Your Kids* (J. McDowell
and D. Day).

British Library Cataloguing in Publication Data
A record for this book is available from the British Library

ISBN 0 340 71006 3

Typeset by Hewer Text Composition Services, Edinburgh
Printed and bound in Great Britain by
Clays Ltd, St Ives plc

Hodder and Stoughton Ltd
A Division of Hodder Headline PLC
338 Euston Road
London NW1 3 BH

For Richard
16th December 1975–25th July 1993

and for his mother, Mary,
and sisters, Amanda and Catherine,
who loved him much

There's a hole in the world now. In the place where he was, there's now just nothing. A centre, like no other, of memory and hope and knowledge and affection which once inhabited the earth is gone. Only a gap remains. A perspective on this world unique in this world which once moved about within this world has been rubbed out. Only a void is left. There's nobody who saw as he saw, knows what he knew, remembers what he remembered, loves what he loved. A person, an irreplaceable person, is gone. Never again will anyone apprehend the world quite the way he did. Never again will anyone inhabit the world the way he did. Questions I have can never now get answers. The world is emptier. My son is gone. Only a hole remains, a void, a gap, never to be filled.

Nicholas Wolterstorff
Lament for a Lost Son

Contents

Acknowledgments

In so many books it is the efforts of the many that have helped and supported the work of the author. There is no difference here. There were those who supported my family and me during our time of grief and whose prayers and gifts were like water in the desert.

John and Pat Haram, who were caring for our son at the time of his death, are among our dearest friends. Ashley and Di Smyth and the people of Stellenburg Chapel were of great support. Financial gifts from the St James' Church Relief Fund; Christ Church, Hillcrest; St Stephen's Church, Claremont; and Peter Gardener, kept bread on the table.

Dan and Hilary Fraser, Ian and Trish Turk, Paul and Barbara Mann, Mike and Cheryl Steele, Mark and Morag Atherstone, Noel Wright and Peter Flagg are just some of the wonderful people that God sent to us in South Africa.

I am indebted to my editor, Annabel Robson of Hodder and Stoughton in London, for her advice, encouragement and longsuffering, to my friend and colleague David Stevens for his careful reading of my manuscript, and

xi

to Rory and Moira McLeod for their valuable support in difficult days.

Mary, Amanda and Catherine, with me here on earth, and Richard, who waits for us in heaven, are more precious to me than life itself.

And thank you, God, for bringing all these people into my life, making me all the richer.

Clive Okill
Abbotsham, August 1997

1

North Devon, 25th July 1993

As a cloud vanishes and is gone,
  so he who goes down to the grave does not return.
  He will never come to his house again;
  his place will know him no more.
                                    (Job 7:9–10)

Shortly after I got up that Sunday morning, I stubbed the little toe of my left foot. It happened as I returned from the bathroom and made my way barefoot back to the bedroom. It was against the leg of a small table and the pain was excruciating. It is amazing how such a small part of the anatomy, when hurt, can incapacitate the whole body. Even my eyes watered. The day was uneventful: after attending possibly one of the worst church services in the history of Christendom, I spent the rest of it hobbling about the garden burning rubbish and cutting back bushes that had encroached upon the drive. At about 4.30 in the afternoon I developed a severe headache, and after a light supper I took an early bath and went to bed at 9.00 p.m. feeling somewhat sorry for myself. It wasn't just because of the aches – I was finding it very difficult to find full-time work as a minister in the Church of England. There were plenty of empty pulpits but, due to what proved to be some unwise financial investment, the Church had found itself short of cash and was unwilling to make new appointments. Later, it transpired that it would become even more difficult for applicants like me, who were returning from overseas. I did have a couple of interviews lined up and was planning a trip to Swindon the following Friday, as well as a meeting with a vicar in North Devon a week later.

It was shortly after ten when the phone rang.

'Dad, it's for you. It's John and he says he must speak to you.' Catherine, our youngest, had taken the call and there seemed an urgency in her voice. John was one of our dearest friends and it was at his home in Cape Town that my son Richard was staying prior to joining us in England.

'Clive, I have some very bad news,' he said. There was a pause.

'Yes, John, what's the matter?' My voice was suddenly grave, which is unusual when speaking to John. We always banter in silly French accents when talking on the phone. We share a common affection for Inspector Clouseau of the *Pink Panther* movies.

'It's very bad news.' By now my wife, Mary, was crouched on her knees in front of me, looking at my face.

'What's the matter?' she asked. 'What's wrong?'

'It's OK, John,' I said, looking intently at my wife as I spoke into the phone, 'just tell me what it is.'

'Richard is dead. There was a terrorist attack on the church this evening and Richard was killed ...' He continued speaking but I couldn't hear the words. Like a wax dummy and a fool I simply handed the phone to Mary. I let him tell her the dreadful news. I sat stunned. I had lost all feeling.

North Devon, 25th July 1993

The news that was about to hit the world's headlines was
appalling. Four armed terrorists had burst into the church
in the middle of a service and simply opened fire with
semi-automatic weapons after lobbing two hand grenades
into a congregation of about twelve hundred people. Eleven
people were killed, including some visiting Russian seamen,
my friend Marita Ackerman and my son Richard. Other
friends had been wounded either by gunshot or shrapnel
in the attack. Large nails had been taped or glued to the
hand grenades. That only eleven people were killed was
a miracle; that one of them was Richard was a question
that was to haunt us. The next five months for our family
were to be aptly described by my younger sister Colleen as
'everyone's worst nightmare'. She was right. We were still
reeling from the collapse of my ministry in Cape Town in
1992, but now as we clung to each other some six thousand
miles away from our son's broken body, we were to begin
pounding on the door of heaven in a way we had never
done before. Perhaps it would be that very pounding and
screaming that would blot out the still small voice of God
as He tried to comfort us. We were to come to believe that
He had stopped His ears to our pleading and turned His
back away.

The telephone began to ring again. Rory, my friend
from London, rang to inform me of the attack as we had
a common link with the church in Cape Town.

'I know about it, Rory,' I said lamely. 'Richard was one of
those killed.' Rory was shattered. Ashley Smyth, who had
helped pastor me through the turbulent months of late 1992,
phoned from his home in Pinelands and burst into tears
when he heard my voice. He had lost a son some years before
and while sharing my grief was reliving some of his own.

3

Now began the hurried task of arranging transport back to South Africa. All flights were full for the next week. Mike Steele, who had been a colleague in the same denomination for many years and once played bass in some of the musicals we had performed, was working for a travel agent and had phoned me, first to share in our loss but second to say he was going to move heaven itself to get us on a plane. He succeeded: after a few 'on and off' long-distance phone calls we were finally told at 9.00 a.m. that South African Airways would take us in the business class section of their 6.00 p.m. flight to Johannesburg. It was the first of many provisions that God would make to soften the blow. My friend Noel Wright had phoned and offered to cover all flight costs – another provision. It was he who told me more of the circumstances of how Richard had died, how he had thrown himself on his two friends, Bonny and Lisa, to protect them, and had taken the force of the bullets.

Mary's brother, Dr John Arkle, and his wife Pauline drove us from Bideford to Heathrow, getting us to the airport with about half an hour to spare. The journey was a sombre one and there was little conversation. I remember asking John how his family had coped when his older brother Charlie had died, killed by a truck when he was eleven. Mary was nine and John was six at the time. John said that he couldn't remember much but that there had been plenty of tears.

On the flight, the relative comfort of business class in no way compensated for the internal conflict of pain and confusion. Although I tried to be physically controlled, tears flowed ceaselessly throughout the night. The loss of Richard was more than enough to deal with; but we had to cope with his death while still coming to terms with

4

the loss of a home, with all our possessions in cardboard boxes, and the loss of employment. The fact that this was a ministry in the Christian Church made it all the more traumatic. On top of all that Mary's father had died only six months earlier. My diary entry for Monday 26th July 1993, which I wrote on the plane, reads as follows:

> Spent all of Sunday night and Monday morning awake and dazed. Catherine took the news badly but later settled down. The phone calls began. John again, David Streater, Roger Williams, Rory Macleod. Travelled to Exeter to meet Amanda at 3.30 a.m. who had come down from Paddington. Tried to doze after getting home. Mike phoned early to tell me we were booked on a flight . . . Took off for S.A. – a devastated family – confused, bewildered, frightened. Richard is gone, we can't believe it – we cry a lot and talk about him. What will God allow next? We are never going to sit around the dining-room table again. No sleep came. I'm not surprised.

If our farewells in London were sad, our greetings in Cape Town were even more so. John Haram had arranged for my mother and sister together with a group of our closest friends to meet us at the airport. I cannot relate the occasion as it defies adequate description. All who were there had to some degree or other supported us through the trauma of a failed ministry and were now picking up more broken pieces. Few words were spoken; just being together was important. A friend had organised accommodation for us at his sister's house, which was empty but furnished, a place of quiet in the eye of the storm. Another of God's provisions. After simply dumping bags and cases, we all went to the scene of devastation and tragedy.

Pews were torn up. There were craters in the floor where hand grenades had exploded. It was now thirty-six hours since the attack, and police and forensic experts were still combing everything, but on the spot where Richard died we gathered together to pray. His blood was on the carpet at our feet. Ashley led us in a short reading from Scripture, and for the first time a feeling of relative peace came over us. It didn't last long: very soon we would have to deal with the press. And later, with God Himself. John had arranged for us to see Richard, the next day, at the police mortuary.

Mary insisted that she see him as he was, not made up or artificial or behind glass windows, and so it was into a spotlessly clean, clinical autopsy room we were led. I must admit at this point that I was greatly moved by the concern and sensitivity of the police on duty. They stayed just long enough to see that we were all right, and then left us alone with our son. He lay on a trolley with a clean white sheet drawn up just below his chin. His eyes were slightly open and his lips very pale. To me, standing behind his shoulders, it looked as if he were sleeping peacefully. There was no sign of any wound. Then I heard it, 'Don't worry, Dad, I knew you'd come.' Of course there was no voice, but my mind raced back to another place and another time. The tears began to flow yet again and I left the room. I knew that Mary wanted to be alone with him, so I stepped out into the rain, thoughts whirling. Why did we leave him alone while we all left for England? If only I hadn't left the ministry. Why did he have to go to church that night? If only I had thought more about my family and less about myself. Why does God allow these things to happen? If . . . If . . . On and on it went. How the mind accuses and the heart defends. If . . . The great imponderable 'if'. That's why, I suppose, it *is* imponderable. It has no solution because it has no substance. If I had been conceived just thirty seconds – no, just one second – before I actually was, I would not be who I am. It is a philosophy that is useless, because it achieves nothing but guilt. To hold myself responsible for Richard's death was to deny the sovereignty of God, to deny that He is the author of life and death. He and none other.

I had a jacket but no head cover and the rain continued to fall. It hid my tears. Eventually, I took cover under an awning and was joined by a very tall young man in a white lab coat. He was the pathologist who had performed the autopsy. He comforted me with the information that it would have been impossible for Richard to have known what hit him. The bullet entered at the base of the head in the occipital lobe and travelled into the centre of the brain. If Richard were standing up when shot, which he wasn't, he would have been dead before he hit the floor. The young doctor was a Christian. As we spoke of our respective faith in Christ, he turned to me and said, 'He [Richard] was singing about Jesus and in the next instant, a twinkling of an eye if you like, he was staring Him in the face. What a prospect.' Together we walked back into the autopsy room. A policewoman had brought Mary a chair and she was sitting with her back to the door. I paused and looked at her, sitting beside her son. Apart from my own grief I was suddenly seized with an overpowering compassion for her. She sat motionless, her hands folded in her lap. What thoughts filled her mind? What memories of her living son, now dead beside her, filled her heart? It is at times like these that a man must measure himself, if not for his own sake then for the sake of his family. That gift so precious, so loved and yet so taken for granted. Gone.

Death, I knew, replaced warmth with coldness, replaced activity with stillness. What I had not known, realised or been prepared for was that death also removed the softness. His spirit was gone, and with its departure only a shell remained. The shell was cold, still and stiff. This was not Richard. The blond hair, the sparkling blue eyes, the lithe vital body with the cheeky smile, that was Richard.

Suddenly, at a glance, one's entire system of values is re-established. All the silver in the world, if it were mine, would be of no use in bargaining with God. Were I to lay it before my wife as a token of my love for her she would push it aside with contempt. Nothing has more value than a human life. Yet men take it so lightly. Men? No, they were no more than boys who pulled the triggers that brought us to this hateful place. Richard was only on loan, placed in our trust for a short while, now returned. I thought of King David as he grieved after the death of an infant son. 'He cannot return to me, but I will go to him.'

Then it was time to go. I was the last to leave the room and as I got to the door, I took one final glance over my shoulder at the now shrouded form of Richard. 'Goodbye, my son.'

The main funeral service was not much more than a large media event, or so it felt to me, as a bereaved person. I am very much aware of the collective response of the Church at large, which was overwhelmingly positive and had a tremendous effect on the media, not to mention the nation. Shortly after the initial shock, an amazing testimony emerged from those most affected, in the lack of bitterness towards the perpetrators of that heinous crime. That is not to say that crime should go unpunished; it was just that the Christian community did not seek to avenge itself. I and my family, while outraged and traumatised, certainly felt protected from the sense of wanting vengeance. It was not the witness of the Christians that was in any way at question. The entire Church was shocked and Christians across all denominations were wounded. If one part of the body is injured then the whole body reacts.

There must have been well over two thousand people at the church as four of the eleven killed were laid to rest. Photographers, television crews and reporters abounded. Security police with semi-automatic weapons were strategically placed in case any political organisation wanted to make a further point while the world looked on. I was just about to enter the main part of the building to take my seat with my family beside my son's casket when Sky News asked for an interview. Photographers walked the long aisles impervious to the prayers. One began to set off her flash at my eighty-year-old mother, and when asked to stop by a friend of mine she retorted that she was 'only doing my job'.

I believe that there is a place for the press in times of tragedy and that they can have a constructive role to play. In a free society the press should not be muzzled. Yet all too often the press report what they want to for the sake of sensationalism, and frequently without compassion. In our case it was often aimed at political expediency. The fact that Richard was born in England and had saved the lives of two girlfriends as they sat together that fateful Sunday

night evoked headlines like 'Devon boy hailed as hero of
Cape Town massacre'. One newspaper, keen to make some
non-theological but strongly political point, produced a
banner headline, 'If my son's death could be a turning
point in the history of South Africa . . . then I'll thank
God for it'. I did use those words, but where the little dots
appear was the real point of my statement, a point lost on
the press. The omitted words were 'and bring people closer
to Christ'. Of course no one wants violence in society, but
if Richard's death was *only* for the good of the country
then I would have considered it a waste of life, as much of
the violence before and since in South Africa has proved
to be. The rest of the interview, which covered an entire
front page, was a collection of misquotes, innuendos and
quasi-political claptrap.

The responsibility of the mass media is still something of a
misunderstood area in our society. While clear, responsible
and investigative journalism, giving a balanced, non-biased
account, can be of great benefit to society, the invasion
of privacy often leads to a great deal of hurt which is
heightened by the event that brought the reporters to the
door in the first place. Often, in the need for competitive
reporting and under pressure from demonstrative editors,
reporters will forget the tragedy and cash in on the tears. On
one occasion I was being interviewed by a television crew.
A question was asked which was slightly out of context to
the rest of the conversation but was designed to evoke a
response. It did. Only later did I discover that one of the
two cameramen had been instructed to zoom in close to
my face so that the reaction could be recorded. It was.

In some cases victims become subjected to inaccurate

and judgmental reporting where character and integrity are impaired and misrepresented for the sake of sensationalism. This serves only to intensify the original trauma and leaves the victim with a sense of greater suffering. It is true that, when under the scrutiny of a skilled reporter, people who are under enough pressure anyway may make comments which later and upon reflection they may regret.

It is possible that the nature of some of the press reporting (but by no means all of it) contributed to the isolation I was later to experience from former colleagues, former parishioners and, to a lesser extent, politicians, resulting in my finally leaving South Africa in late 1993 and returning to England. With hindsight, I can see that this was God's tool to aid recovery and not hinder it; I received more pastoral care, more respite and much better job prospects in England than I would ever have received in South Africa. At the time, all I knew was that I had lost my position as a clergyman and, as a result, my home; I had lost my son to terrorists, then my country due to the indifference of others, and all in six months. But it wasn't all bad. Let me start at the beginning.

2

Life under Apartheid

When I was a child, I talked like a child, I thought like a child, I reasoned like a child.
(1 Cor. 13:11)

I was born in Cape Town in 1948, in the same town and the same year that apartheid was born or, more accurately, put on the statute books in South Africa. While it is true to say that it was not law before 1948, it was certainly practised. There was a philosophy of living apart and treating differently the people of other colours and creeds. Virtually my entire life was lived under that system. As a child I knew nothing of it, living in the protection of an affluent white middle-class suburb of Cape Town called Camps Bay, far removed from the sights and sounds of suffering.

Camps Bay is idyllic. It is, as the name suggests, on the coast, and the white sands of the beaches are fringed with palm trees. A range of mountains called the Twelve Apostles rises almost right out of the sea, giving the choice of going swimming or climbing mountains, and almost always in the glorious sunshine of the southern tip of Africa. For a child it was paradise. School work was a hindrance to the activity of any normal young boy in those circumstances.

12

Most of my days were spent either on the beach, exploring the little coves and finding maritime treasures like crabs, shells and flotsam, or in the foothills, defending the land from sea-borne attack with an air-gun.

On one occasion, when I was about eleven, I found a sheet of corrugated iron on a junk heap. I had seen a drawing in a book I was reading of how a young boy, living on the island of Corfu, had built a canoe out of just such material. Dragging the cumbersome sheet home, I planned to do the same and put to sea. What followed was some weeks of clandestine banging, shaping and cursing as the unwilling metal was bent into something that resembled a canoe. The transom was a piece of board around which the iron was bent and nailed. The bow was brought together with a much smaller piece of wood and held in place with several rusty two-inch nails, many of which were bent and some of which stuck through the one-inch piece of wood. These were then flattened with a couple of swipes of the hammer. The joints were sealed with tar that I had pinched from some road men doing repairs to the driveway of a neighbour's house, and all the nail holes were filled in the same way to make it as watertight as possible. I had placed a stay amidships which would serve as a seat and provide some comfort from the unforgiving corrugations that made up the hull. That this would raise the centre of gravity did not occur to me. Everything was done in complete secrecy in a back corner of our very large garden, away from what most certainly would be the disapproval of my father, the horror of my over-protective mother and the scorn and ridicule of my younger sister. I was even reluctant to tell any of my friends for fear of discouragement and mockery.

I had decided that my craft should be black and silver

and named after the Greek god of the sea, Poseidon, and managed to persuade my dad that I needed some silver paint for a school project. I had found a large tin of matt black paint in a box in our garage; it was so old that the rusted lid took some effort to prise off, but enough liquid lay beneath a thick skin of dry paint for my purpose. I had broken the head off what I thought was an old disused broom so that I could use the long handle as a paddle. To each end I attached pieces of plywood from an apple box, again with two-inch nails and some string. The handle was painted black, as was the hull, while the blades of the paddle were silver like the transom and bow. The name *Poseidon* was only on one side as I had begun to run out of silver paint; my father had bought only a very small tin for my project, and on top of that I had kicked it over, spilling most of the contents in the garden. I suppose that, in all, the task took about two months, but finally it was done. All that was needed was to transport the vessel to the coast and fame would be assured. For this task I needed to secure the help of a friend, as the craft was far too heavy for me to carry on my own, even though the beach was less than a quarter of a mile away. It had to be someone who would not blow the gaff and tell anyone else. Not yet at any rate.

'That'll never float.' Gavin looked stoically at my design. The day for the launch had arrived.

'Yes it will!' I said defensively. 'Then you'll want a go as well.'

'It's going to sink, I know it will. My dad's got a boat and I know.' He spoke with some authority and I felt a pang of uncertainty. His dad did have a boat, I had been on it several times and almost always got seasick.

'Well, you don't have to help me, then. I'll just do it myself.' But together we balanced *Poseidon* on my bike between saddle and handlebars and set off down the hill.

As luck would have it we ran into Jeffrey Cohen, a classmate, one who was not known to keep a secret and whose nose constantly dripped. He was standing in the garden of his house, watering the grass with a hosepipe.

'What's that thing?' he demanded. 'Where are you going with it?'

'Oke's going to put it in the sea and sail across to Robben Island,' shouted Gavin. Cohen let out a sound of something between disbelief and laughter as he wiped his nose with the back of his hand.

'This I gotta see,' he said, and leaving the hose running he ran off to fetch Robbie Giles who lived next door. 'It'll never float, you know,' he called over his shoulder as he sneezed and disappeared through a hedge.

I was beginning to wish that we had taken the longer route to the beach as it was less likely that we would have met anyone we knew. But now the die was cast, and we still had to pass the sports field. I was hoping that no one I knew would be there but as I and most of my friends played there almost every day the chances were remote. By the time we finally reached the beach, *Poseidon* was being carried aloft by four stout volunteers, with Gavin pushing my bike and me clutching my paddles. We were followed and surrounded by some fourteen or fifteen noisy eleven-year-olds, all in search of excitement, if not a good laugh.

It was one of those idyllic Cape Town days. There was no wind and the sun beat down on us as we made our way across the white beach with the 'Whites Only' signs along its perimeter. The sand had the unusual property of squeaking beneath your feet and was very hot, causing the little band of boys, browned by the sun and chattering like monkeys with the expectation of something different, to hop from one foot to the other. By now many of them had changed their tune and were vying for a chance to try the craft out for themselves.

The water on the Cape Town west coast is cold. Very cold. The Benguela Current is fed from Antarctica. At times it is so cold that one's feet ache from the shock. And soon we were there, at the appointed site for launching, a quiet cove with a sort of rock jetty protected from the waves. *Poseidon* was carefully placed on to the water. She floated! In fact, when left on her own she produced only a very slight list to port. Fifteen pairs of eyes stared at the bottom of the boat expectantly.

'It doesn't leak,' said David Slade, who had asked if he could be second in line to try her out.

'Not a drop.' For the first time since arriving at the beach I spoke. 'I told you it wouldn't.' My confidence was restored. Even Manfred Jacob, who had been the most cynical of the bunch, was impressed. 'Gavin is next after me,' I said, now with complete authority, 'because he helped carry it the furthest. Keith, hold the bow, and Robbie, hold the stern while I get in.'

'What's the bow?' asked Keith as he withdrew a finger from his ear and wiped it on his shirt.

'The front end, you fool,' said Gavin, who was holding her steady amidships, 'the front.' Keith almost slipped into the water as he grabbed the bow, but finally all was ready for me. The water was deep and dark at the point of launch, so there would be no snagging or hindrances and departure would be smooth. I climbed aboard and

16

sat down on the centre stay. Still she did not leak. Not a drop.

'Pass the paddles, Jeff,' I said, as I settled my backside on to the makeshift seat. 'Right, push her off, Robbie.' Robbie gave *Poseidon* a gentle push and I dug one blade of the paddle into the water. I felt a slight wobble beneath me – and then she capsized. She just turned completely on her side, filled with water and sank like a stone. Even though I was a good swimmer, the freezing water took my breath away and I disappeared from sight.

'He's drowned!' screamed Jeffrey as his nose ran more profusely than before.

'Don't be daft,' said Thomas, 'there he is.' I surfaced, spluttering and gasping, as frenzied hands reached out to me amid howls of derision. Robbie Giles was weeping with laughter and holding on to his sides in the discomfort of uncontrolled humour.

'It sank, it sank!' he hooted. The others joined in the chorus as I was dragged dripping on to the rocks. I felt like a fool. My pride was more than dented, it was destroyed. I picked up the paddles, which were all that remained of my venture, and walked away. *Poseidon* was nowhere to be seen, lost for ever beneath the depths. To this day she remains beneath the sea, a rusting, barnacle-encrusted relic of an eleven-year-old schoolboy's dream of adventure and fame. I walked across the scorching sand and up the road, dragging my paddle and leaving a trail of sea water behind.

'What did yo do wid my blerrie brroom?' Joanie, our coloured maid, demanded as she snatched the paddles from my hand. 'Yor mudder is going to kilt yo wen I tells her.' She removed a hand from her hip and aimed a swipe at my ear. I ducked and the blow glanced off the top of my head. She had been searching for the broom for some time, doing most of her sweeping with brush and pan.

Before I went to bed that night, I looked down at the beach from the upstairs balcony of our house. The heat of the day was gone and a cold wind blew up from the sea, causing me to pull my dressing-gown around my chest. I could just see the white tops of the waves as they broke over the sands and thought of the little craft that now lay beneath the dark waters. I shivered. *Poseidon* had taken several weeks to build, but had been taken from me in a matter of seconds. I don't remember, but I probably cried myself to sleep.

A few days later, and twenty-two days before my twelfth birthday, on 21st March 1960 sixty-nine black people were killed by police in the little-known town of Sharpeville. I remember looking at the newspaper photographs of the bodies lying in the street with uniformed policemen standing among them, 'They *must* have been trying to cause trouble,' I thought to myself. 'Why else would they have been shot dead?' Casual comments, from an essentially uncaring community and especially eleven-year-old schoolboys who had heard parental conversations at home, seemed to confirm these thoughts. 'They were trying to cause a riot,' said one. 'I heard that they attacked a police station,' said another. Why would they want to do that, I thought to myself; surely most people in this country were happy and content? In our kitchen, Joanie had become more silent than usual. In other kitchens across the country, there were tears. The truth, as was to emerge much later, was that the people killed were among a group who had peacefully demonstrated outside

Sharpeville police station. It was the police who panicked and opened fire on unarmed human beings. I was not to discover that for many years.

Overnight there was a change, one that was tangible across the nation. Blacks began to stay away from work and the government reacted with great severity. The ANC and the PAC were declared illegal organisations. Thousands were detained and later sentenced to prison. Prime Minister Verwoerd called a state of emergency. Soldiers were deployed along the main roads that entered Cape Town and especially around the townships of Langa and Gugeletu. For me it was a time of relative excitement as I used to watch the troop carriers and armed soldiers patrolling the streets. They were all white and I felt a sense of security. Surely, nobody would mess with them.

Nobody did, but a few weeks later someone took a shot at the Prime Minister at an open-air show, wounding him severely in the head. He survived, only to succumb to an assassin's knife six years later, in 1966, as he took his seat in parliament.

I suppose I became more alarmed, two years after Sharpeville, at the crisis that was developing on the other side of the Atlantic around the island of Cuba. It is interesting how one's youthful opinions are formed by the comments of one's parents. 'That idiot Kennedy will kill us all,' was my father's remark one Saturday as he picked up the *Cape Times*. And because he was my father, I believed him to be right. His comments about the situation in South Africa were less forthcoming. He was too busy trying to keep his printing business going to be worried about detentions without trial. I was too busy trying to avoid homework and make the first team in rugby.

Most English-speaking white people who are today ten years either side of fifty and who lived as teenagers in South Africa in the 1960s and 1970s will speak now of their opposition to apartheid. In reality, if they were honest, they didn't care much at the time. There were those who left the country, to fight this regime from abroad. There were some who remained to voice their opposition and take the consequences of what was essentially a police state, and there were those who grappled with God in prayer for change, but they were in the minority. For the main part, most were silent. They would be unlikely to admit it today, but they got on with the good life. And it was carried on the backs of the black majority. The number of Afrikaans-speaking Whites who stood in opposition to the government could be counted on the fingers of your hands. The beatings, the arrests, the detentions without trial, the abuse of the workforce continued. As for me, a skinny, acne-bespotted, politically ignorant teenager, the first team was all that mattered. I had to make the first team. And I did.

Being a teenager in South Africa in the 1960s was great. It was the age of the Beatles and the Stones, and of experimenting with things our parents never did. The two major influences in my life at the time were sport and the beach. I went to church most Sundays, but it was more under duress than through conviction, as my mother was the driving force in this area, 'driving' being the operative word. Almost as if it was her conscience that was being put at ease, I had to be confirmed at thirteen and serve as an altar boy in the little Anglican church in Camps Bay, even though I had not the slightest notion of what I was

20

doing or why I was doing it. In all the years I attended this church I don't remember the gospel preached, even once. Even here apartheid was not mentioned.

One Sunday morning, when I dutifully arrived at church I was grabbed by Ernest, the senior altar boy. His name was a fitting description of his attitude, especially to church matters.

'Grant can't make it this morning, so you will have to stand in for him at the altar.' I was aghast. My moment had arrived. Together with David Barnewall, I had been training, under Ernest's watchful eye, to be one of the next generation of acolytes. I donned my robes.

'Gosh, you're lucky,' said David, as we lined up for procession. I was quick to note his look of envy. He was in the front with those lesser mortals, the choir, while I was at the back, carrying a huge candle in a wooden holder. I almost swelled with pride. The minister, Father Walters, winked at me as we began to move into the church. My parents and the entire local Christian community had their eyes fixed on *me*. The service depended on my ability to do things right – lifting the candle at the right time, ringing the bell at the magic words and helping with the bread and wine. Of course, I, together with Bobby, the other, much older acolyte, would be served communion first, ahead of the common people in the pews.

All went according to plan. But, alas, there came a point in the service when Bobby and I were required to remain on our knees for a protracted period of time. This we had not rehearsed before. And while my knees withstood the strain, my sense of duty did not. It was a communion service and naturally I had omitted breakfast that morning.

My head began to swim. The world began to take on

a lighter shade of grey. Soon the altar and its ornaments were dancing before my eyes. I leaned heavily against the candlestick. I tried to breathe more evenly. I tried to wiggle my toes so that my oxygen-starved brain might receive more blood. Why I had the presence of mind to do that, I do not know. But all was to no avail: I began to topple over. Bobby came to my rescue and I was ignominiously dragged from the sanctuary. David Barnewall took my place.

'You are allowed to eat breakfast,' Father Walters told me later. But I felt as if I had let him down.

'If joo doesn't work at skool, den joo's gonna be a rubbis like me an only work in de gartden.' This advice came from Basil Smart, an ebony-skinned man of about fifty who worked for my dad as a general assistant at his printing business and sometimes earned a bit of extra cash by helping out in the garden. He had brilliant teeth, all the whiter against his dark skin. I had taken him some refreshment one Saturday when he was toiling away in our backyard under the hot sun. He took the tin mug of tea and enamel plate of brown bread and peanut butter and sat on the grass beside an ancient lawn mower. Frankly I felt it would have been quicker to cut the grass with a pair of eyebrow tweezers than to use that piece of antiquity. I sat down beside him and sipped my Coke from a tall glass. His eating utensils were always kept separate from the rest of the family's, as were Joanie's. I remember thinking about this from time to time, but never questioned my mother. It was just the way things were.

'I hate school, Basil,' I said. 'I just don't seem to be doing things right. I mean, just this week a teacher told me, in front of the class, that the only time I would be of any

22

use to anyone would be if I gave my body to the hospital.'
Basil roared with laughter and the bread sputtered from
his lips. 'That's just how the class reacted,' I said ruefully.
'They all laughed.' I pulled at the grass.

'Even Bridget?' he asked. He knew of my crush on a
girl with blonde hair and legs up to her armpits.

'Even Bridget,' I said.

'Masser mussen worry. Joo's OK, Masser.' Even then I
hated that title. I wasn't his master. I wasn't even my own
master. I had just set the school record for the lowest grade
in maths in standard eight – 7 per cent. But I had made
the first team. And at sixteen that wasn't too bad a feat.
'Masser mus jus work a bit harder. Joo'll be all right.' I
liked Basil and enjoyed talking to him. He had once advised
me on how to ask a girl out on a date. 'Joo jus goes ups to
her an says, "Hey dol, let's go groove." Dis can't fail wid
de chicks,' he assured me. I never followed his advice and
from what I later learnt about the fairer sex, I am very glad
I didn't. I would like to think that Basil is still alive today,
although this is unlikely given his propensity to drink. I
suppose it helped him forget the squalor of his home after
he had left the luxury of ours.

This fact struck me strongly one year when my father
gave Basil a five-kilogram gas bottle, with a stainless-steel
cooking ring. His eyes shone with delight.

'Now I can go an get me a lekker baat.' He meant he
could now enjoy a hot bath in an iron tub at home by
heating the water on the gas ring. All I had to do was
turn a tap.

Some thirty years later, in 1994, I stood in the long line
of expatriate South Africans outside South Africa House,
waiting to vote in the first fully democratic election. I

recall one middle-class white person in the queue being interviewed by a news reporter, saying, 'We [notice the collective pronoun] have been working and waiting for this day for many years now. I'm glad that it is now all over and full democracy has come to South Africa.' It was a load of twaddle, as the person concerned had no intention of returning to the country and had most certainly made little, if any, effort to eradicate apartheid himself.

3

A Peace from the Moon

In righteousness I shall see your face;
   when I awake, I shall be satisfied

(Ps. 17:15)

Mary and I were separated by some six thousand miles when our second child, Richard, was born on 16th December 1975. Unlike the birth of his sister, Amanda, in 1972, I missed his entry into the world and was not to see him until he was six months old.

I had met his mother on a blind date in 1968 in Cape Town, and married her in a little church in Shirwell, North Devon, England, in 1970. (She takes delight in reminding me that she was 'blind' and I was the date.) During this time in our lives there had been a complicated series of moves back and forth between South Africa and England and Richard, having been conceived at our home in Cape Town, was born in England while Mary was staying with her parents in Devon.

We were just like any other struggling couple in their twenties, trying to start a home and a family on limited resources. We had our moments of triumph as well as of tears. I was working for a pharmaceutical company as a medical representative, travelling the length and breadth of the west coast of South Africa. We went to church now and then, but the 'now and then' was usually restricted to Easter and Christmas as I was about as spiritual as a bag of cement. In the sense that we went twice a year, we were regulars. But all that was about to change.

Whenever I was away from home on lengthy business trips, I would buy the family little gifts to mark my return. On one of these occasions I bought Mary a small cross, as she used to collect gold charms. Like anything else, I thought that the trinket was of little significance other than its face value which, given time, would appreciate.

'How interesting,' she exclaimed as she and the children opened their gifts, 'as there is something I have to tell you.' I looked at her across the dinner table. 'While you were away I became a Christian.' She fingered the cross.

I was completely unfazed by the remark. 'Thought you always were one,' I muttered through a mouthful of spaghetti.

'So did I. And I probably was, only –' she paused to wipe the food from Richard's cheek and chin and eyebrows '– only your sister and I went to a church and I gave my life to the Lord.' By now I had stopped eating and was staring at her. This was an entirely different matter. This was an entirely different terminology. '*Gave myself to the Lord.*' What did she mean by giving herself to the Lord? This was the language of the seriously deranged religious freaks. I grunted, thinking to myself that it was just a phase, like the vegetarian one, and it would soon pass. 'You should come with us next Sunday,' she continued, 'they have a band and the people are very friendly.'

'I'm sure they are.' By now I was getting defensive.

'You know I can't go on a Sunday, because of Tarus,' I muttered. Never before did training our German Shepherd dog look so appealing, no matter what the weather. A band, indeed! What kind of church would have a band? Only the hand-waving, eyeball-rolling, frothing-at-the-mouth, falling-on-the-ground, wrist-slashing type. I shivered and put the plates in the sink.

The weeks that followed were different, to say the least. Mary did not behave as if she had stepped off another planet, but instead seemed quite normal. If there was any difference, it was for the better. She seemed calmer – not that she was ever the stressful type, but there was a sort of tranquillity about her. She seemed better able to cope, and managed the household affairs, as well as the children, with much more maturity. She and my sister Colleen would go off to church every Sunday morning and evening, as well as attending a mid-week Bible study which was run by Barry van Eyssen, a man I once used to work with. He had always seemed quite normal and rational to me when we had had dealings in the past, and it was from my beer-swigging, crude colleagues that I learnt that Barry was some sort of religious weirdo. I certainly never got that impression from him. Maybe it was because they had heard he went to church, or something. I even played my part in the spiritual development of my wife and younger sister by lending them my new Audi to travel to church and back. Very magnanimous.

On only one occasion I flipped. It was one evening when we all sat down to supper. Mary dutifully placed a plate of food in front of me and the children, then sat down without serving herself.

'What's the matter?' I asked, 'Are you OK?'

'I'm fine,' she replied.

'Why aren't you eating with us? Are you sure you are all right?'

'Yes,' she said, 'I'm just fasting.' She smiled.

I looked at her and stopped eating. 'What?'

'Fasting. You know, going without food for a short time during prayer.' This was definitely over the top. Not only had her language become weird, but now her actions were fanatical. This was what mad people did when going on some sort of religious pilgrimage, never to be seen again.

'Listen,' I said, pointing a fork at her as a fear of the unknown suddenly engulfed me, 'if you want to starve yourself to death, that's OK with me. Just make sure that there is food in front of me and my kids.' Strange how possessive one becomes when self-righteousness takes hold. Only a few hours earlier I had told Mary to clean up *her* son's nappy as it was leaking into his cot.

'You won't starve,' she smiled, 'I'll see to that.'

'You should come with us one day,' my sister said, 'you really would enjoy it.'

'Yeah, I'm sure I would. But the dog needs training and someone's got to do it.'

'Why don't you come for just three weeks in a row? Then we won't bother you any more,' suggested Mary. They spent some time trying to convince me that it really would be good for me to go with them. But the dog needed training.

Then it happened. It rained. For days the heavens opened and poured their contents on to the ground. The field we used for training our dogs was deluged. I was sunk. I didn't have any excuse not to go with them to church. 'All right,'

28

I reluctantly agreed, 'but only for three weeks, and then you must leave me alone.'

'Promise,' said the two of them together, but as I left the room I was certain I heard one of them say, '*Yes.*'

'Anything wrong?' I asked as I stuck my head back around the door.

'No, everything's fine,' said Mary, looking as if she had just gone to heaven and discovered it was made of Devonshire clotted cream. 'Go and watch telly and I'll bring you some tea.' This was strange: Mary *never* encouraged me to watch telly.

The building was unimpressive and functional. There were no ornaments, altar or stained glass windows. It didn't look like a church at all. In fact, it was quite unlike anything I had been accustomed to. The people were friendly. They actually smiled when you entered the door, and seemed genuinely pleased to see you. There was no stifled silence as you sat down, only a sense of expectancy. People actually talked to each other. And there was a band. Five or six musicians played a couple of pleasant-sounding items before someone stood up at the front and invited us to sing a few choruses along with them.

The singing was outstanding; it had rhythm and life. Nobody fell on the floor or ran about in a bizarre way muttering unintelligible noises, and on top of that I was struck by the well-ordered way the service was conducted. There was no long, intoned recitation from a prayer book, and most unusually, to me at any rate, there was a soloist, Glenda, who sang a very beautiful song in an equally beautiful voice.

The sermon lasted about thirty minutes and was preached

by a man in his early thirties called Frank Retief. He didn't wear any robes and had an Elvis Presley hairstyle. Initially, I was surprised by his voice because, although a little high-pitched, it was normal and conversational, unlike the sonorous baritones of the sombre High-Church style that had been my somewhat limited experience to date. I had heard it said that this particular preacher was a man with a message and an outstanding speaker. He proved to be both, and in only a few moments I was caught up in what he was saying. For the first time in my life I heard of a God who loves us and actually cared enough to enter our world and be a real living part of it. I heard of a God who died for my sins and was in fact prepared to forgive me of them. I had never heard anything like it before. Although I didn't realise it then, it was this man's ministry which was to affect my own.

It was all very different that Sunday morning and I did feel somewhat intimidated by the appeal at the end of the service, that if anyone wanted to be forgiven, they could put their hand up and someone would pray for them. This I felt I couldn't do. I was not about to make a public spectacle of myself.

It is strange that when God is moving you into a corner you are not apparently aware of it, although odd things start to happen. One day, in a local supermarket, I happened to meet Bruce Stenmann, a former workmate who could drink and party with the best of them. We had not seen each other for some time. I was delighted. As we exchanged greetings I noticed that Bruce was much more reserved than usual. He almost had an air of peace and tranquillity.

'Well, buddy,' I said, 'still slogging it out in the world

of commerce and industry?' I was trying to make small talk.

'Actually, no, Clive,' he said. 'I'm going to theological college next month. I'm going to become a priest. I've received Jesus as my Lord and Saviour.' My mouth dropped open. This was the language of my wife. Bruce, religious? I was stunned.

'That's wonderful, Bruce,' I muttered. I had very nearly knocked a pyramid of baked beans into the aisles. 'Er, I've got to meet Mary. She's also found Jesus.' His face lit up, and I fled. Wherever I turned I was meeting those I once knew as ordinary people who were now finding religion – past school chums, workmates and sports pals. There seemed no escape. God was dealing with me in His own deliberate way.

'Why don't you come with me to hear him speak?' my dad asked. He had just received two tickets to hear Jim Irwin, lunar module pilot on Apollo 15, give an address at a Rotary luncheon in Cape Town. Jim had been giving some talks about his trip to the moon as well as taking a number of church meetings. He was a born-again Christian and was speaking of his faith as well as his love of space. I was intrigued.

'OK,' I said, 'I'll come.' I remember the unpretentious meal at a five-star hotel – the avocado pear was under-ripe – but I don't remember too much about Jim's talk. However, we were invited to purchase his autobiography, *To Rule the Night*, and he offered to sign copies. I went forward and asked him to sign my book, and after endorsing it he shook my hand. We chatted.

'My wife is also called Mary,' he said, as he held my gaze.

I was struck by the utter calm and peace that surrounded him. Here was a man who had flown to and walked on the moon, and yet he took the time to pass on to me the things that mattered to him. That night I went and sat down on the beach not far from my house and watched the waves wash the shore. In the distance was the silhouette of a moonlit Table Mountain. I wanted the peace that Jim had, the peace that Bruce had and the peace that Mary had found. I wanted it badly.

I don't think that I ever rose to the three-week challenge that had been set before me by my wife and sister. It was two weeks and a few days after that first visit to the church in Kenilworth that I sat on my bed and told Mary that I wanted to have what she had. Her reaction was simple.

'Ask God to forgive you and for Jesus to have control of your life.'

'What, here? Now?'

'Yes.'

'Don't you have to be in church or something?' I was moving into procrastination mode.

'Nope, here will do nicely.' She sat down beside me.

'I don't know what to say.'

'That makes a change,' she chided, then, holding my hand, she looked at me. 'Just say whatever comes into your head. God understands. He's been around a bit longer than you, you know.' Mary's ability with logic has always been alarming.

'Do I have to shut my eyes?' I must have sounded pleading. But don't forget, I was a trained acolyte. I knew all there was to know about ritual. I had even carried the cross for the Archbishop of Cape Town. That must count for something.

'No,' she said, 'as long as you mean it and are not saying it just to please me.'

'Lord,' I began, 'I'm sorry I've been a sinner and messed up so much. And I'm not very good at this sort of thing, so forgive me for messing up even now as I speak, but I know that you can forgive because Jesus died on the cross for my sake, as well as other people's, but it's really me I'm asking for and would you please forgive and help me be a better husband and dad and I really need you to have a bit more control of my life, so would you, please, and I don't really know what else to say now, so thank you. Amen.' I looked at Mary. I'm not sure even to this day if she was about to laugh or cry. 'Is that it?' I asked.

'Yes,' she said, 'that's it.'

'But I don't feel any different,' I said, somewhat disappointed.

'What did you want, fireworks and cannon shot?'

'Worked for St Paul,' I replied.

'Well, St Clive, there is something you have to do.' I knew there was a trick. 'You have to tell someone.' She smiled. 'It will help confirm it in your mind.' My mind! It was racing. Whom could I tell? I had visions of all my work colleagues falling about, laughing their heads off, pointing and weeping with mirth like the day *Poseidon* sank. No, I couldn't tell them. Barry! That was it! I would tell Barry van Eyssen. He wouldn't laugh. We had worked together some years before. He was a Christian and now ran a Bible study at the church Mary had taken me to. Alas, he couldn't come to the phone as he was in the bath, but would return my call in a little while. Well, a little while turned into a long while and two hours later, at about eleven that night,

33

I climbed into my own steaming tub. The phone rang. Of course it was Barry.

'I'll phone him tomorrow,' I yelled from the security of the bath.

'No you won't,' said Mary, 'now or never.' And standing, clad only in a towel, dripping water on to the carpet, I told a delighted Barry that I had become a Christian.

For me, there was no strange and wonderful sensation that accompanied my new-found faith. There was no sense of having the great weight of sin removed, no weeping with relief or joy or any of the experiences that some say they feel upon trusting in Christ. I just got on with life. I continued to go to work and do my job and see my friends. Just everyday things. It was, however, brought to my attention that my language had improved, when my secretary commented one day that I had stopped using strong words. I was somewhat surprised. I hadn't noticed it. It was as if it were completely natural not to swear. I do remember hedging a bit when she asked me why, and found myself admitting that it probably had something to do with me going to church on Sundays.

'But I thought that you trained your dog on Sunday,' she said. I smiled wistfully.

There was no quick grasp of matters spiritual as the months passed, but often things I had heard said or preached struck home, like long-lost chords. 'Where have I heard that before?' I often asked myself. Gradually old hymns and bits of the 1662 Book of Common Prayer that I could recall from my youth seem to creep into my mind. 'We acknowledge and bewail our manifold sins and wickedness, which we, from time to time, most grievously have committed . . .'

There it was. I now knew how men like Thomas Cranmer felt. This was not just a boring old document which people intoned mindlessly. Well, it was if you let it, but there was a depth of spiritual passion that I had had access to but had never realised. I read the ancient Creeds again. 'I believe in one God the Father Almighty, Maker of heaven and earth . . . I look for the resurrection of the dead, and the life of the world to come.' Hey! Wait a bit, I believe that too. The Magnificat: I had sung it, or intoned it mindlessly, countless times. 'My soul doth magnify the Lord and my spirit doth rejoice in God my saviour.' These were Mary's words when she heard of the pending birth of her son Jesus. They were now also mine. For me a link with the past had become so real. I have always loved historical connections, and now I was part of a history, tradition and family that went back to creation. Jesus's God was my God, my Father, and therefore my family. I felt as if I belonged. The peace that moon man Jim Irwin had and Bruce Stenmann had and Mary had, I now felt. And it wasn't a bad feeling.

4

Where Choirs and Angels . . .

*It is better to take refuge in the LORD
than to trust in man.*

(Ps. 118:8)

The year that followed was swallowed up in activity. I
became involved in a church drama group and then the
music ministry. The church and its leadership encouraged
a rather unorthodox approach to services – at least I thought
it was unorthodox, and I was quite happy to go along. I
was now attending church twice on a Sunday, as well as a
mid-week Bible study. There was nothing fanatical about
what we did and we all enjoyed doing it. Well, I thought
that there was nothing fanatical about it; I'm sure that some
of my old friends and workmates would have thought that
going to church once a week was a bit over the top, let
alone three times! In fact, it turned out to be four or five
times if you took into account the band practices. Yes,
it had to happen: I got involved with the band, playing
keyboards.

It was a little after joining the band that I began to explore
my somewhat limited musical ability. I had played the piano
from the age of about six or seven until I was seventeen. At
first I had studied the classics, and then moved on to jazz

and modern syncopation. But you must remember where I grew up. The beach, the sport and the girls in my life had a much stronger attraction than a set of ivory keys, and so I gave up playing in favour of the things just described.

'You will regret it later,' my mother admonished me.

'Yeah, yeah,' was my truculent reply. She was right, of course, but I was not to discover that for a few years. Now, as a Christian, I was keen to play in the band. I would have to practise again.

A turning point came when we, as a church, decided to produce a children's musical called *Cool in the Furnace*, an American work about Daniel in the lions' den. A local music teacher was approached to work the score and put a small orchestra together. It was brilliant. I was hooked, and when it was all over I began to set about developing my own choir, consisting of young adults whom I asked to join in. In those early days the group was about fifteen strong. Little did I ever dream that we would grow to a force of about eighty – and on one occasion one hundred and twenty – singers, performing on radio and national television. For now, fifteen was good enough.

Saturday morning. Lie-in time. All quiet, all right with the world. No running battles from the children's part of the house as Amanda, our eldest, was staying overnight at her Ouma's (Grandma's) flat in Sea Point. Her two-year-old brother Richard was sleeping soundly in his bed without a care in the world. I turned over and looked at the red glow of the digital clock beside the bed: 8.05. We had got in late the night before and were trying to sleep off the effects of the long hours we had kept with choir and orchestra practice. We were finally ready for the first performance of a musical drama, called *The Way*. It was a first for me and quite naturally I was excited about the prospect of seeing the endeavour going on stage before an audience of some eight hundred people the next day. The musical had taken nine months to write and arrange, and had been done on and off as I had journeyed around the country as a medical representative for a large pharmaceutical company. There is not much one can do between towns on long hauls of many hours' travel except daydream, listen to the radio or be creative in one's thinking. I listened to the radio a lot, but most of the time I tried to be creative. I half sat up in bed with the music very much alive in my head. It was simple stuff but I had written it myself and felt good about it. A musical account of the life of Christ crammed into forty-five minutes. A story that, if it were fully told, not all the books in the world could contain. But I had done it in forty-five minutes. And put it to music.

It was awfully quiet in the other part of the house. Even if Amanda was away, Richard by now should be creating some havoc of his own. Through my blurred vision – I have an eye condition called kerataconus or, if you like, bulging corneas – I looked again at my digital clock: 8.10. It was too quiet. Mary slept soundly beside me, so I decided to see what mischief the little terrorist was silently up to. Plodding down the passage I noticed that his door was open. Not a sound came from the room.

'Richard, what are you do–?' I entered the room. It was empty! Bedclothes were dishevelled, toys scattered. Everything was completely normal except he wasn't there. Turning towards his sister's room, a place he was well known to frequent and destroy, I opened the door. It was undisturbed, except for the fact that the window, which was a long one from floor to ceiling, was wide open. 'Mary,' I called out as I quickly moved from room to room, 'Mary, Richard's gone! MARY!' My wife must have registered the panic in my voice because she was by my side in an instant.

'What do you mean, gone? He must be here! Did you look out the back?'

I tore at the back door. Tarus, our German Shepherd, looked at me with more than passing interest as I burst into the large enclosed yard. Empty. No Richard.

'He's not here,' I yelled.

'Clive,' she called, 'he's not in the house. Something has happened. I've found his nappy.' It was still pinned together and soiled and had been lying on the floor of his bedroom. Often this article of clothing fell down his little legs as he began to grow out of the need of it. Now he only wore it at night and the wet weight would often not be supported by the pins as he got up in the morning. He would simply step out of the hindrance to his daily task of plunder and mayhem, and leave the offending deposit on the floor. But now he was nowhere to be found. We were petrified.

'Oh God, I'll look out the front.' That should have been the first and obvious choice as the open window led on to the front garden, which in turn was open to the street. I was down the road in a moment, clad only in my pyjama bottoms. Lex, my neighbour, stared wide-eyed at the apparition before him. 'Lex, Richard is missing. Have you seen him?' He shook his head. 'Somehow he has got out, and we don't know where he is.' This is a parent's worst nightmare. We didn't know how long he had been gone, where he was or indeed if he had been stolen in the night. These things did happen. Lex saw the terror in my face.

'Go that way. I'll go up the street.' He dropped his garden hose on the grass and ran up the road. I still have a picture of that hose twisting and snapping under the pressure. Water caught me full in the upper part of my pyjamas. I was now half-naked and drenched in all the wrong places – hardly the attire for a public appearance in my own neighbourhood. But that didn't even cross my mind. I charged down the road calling my son's name at the top of my voice. Startled motorists took evasive action. Curtains drew back.

Some ten minutes later I returned home in defeat, my feet bleeding, my heart heavy. Mary and Lex were talking calmly on the front porch. Were they mad? Our son had been stolen and they were so calm.

'We found him.' Mary looked at me calmly as she held out a cup of coffee to my bemused neighbour. 'You'd better get changed, you look terrible. I've phoned the police. They know where he is.'

'Where is he?' I demanded. Where was he? What had happened? The POLICE? Why hadn't I thought of the police?

'I'll bring the mug back later,' said Lex, 'I'll just finish my watering.' Chuckling to himself he crossed my lawn.

Richard had woken up at about 6.30 that morning and, stepping out of his hindrance, had made his way to his sister's room, bent on plunder as usual. Discovering her absence he remembered that she was spending the night at Ouma's house. This was a place he would rather be, so clad only in an undersized T-shirt, under which protruded his belly button and everything below it, he had opened the bedroom window and embarked on a journey which he believed would lead him to his elder sister. The fact that my mother lived about forty minutes' drive from where we lived never entered his head. He wanted to find his sister. He had managed to walk undetected for about ten minutes before an elderly gentleman standing in his garden picked him up and took him indoors. Richard's vocabulary at this stage in his life was somewhat limited and he was unable to tell the man or his wife where he lived. They phoned the police.

At nine thirty that Saturday morning they stood at our doorway, an admonishing look on their faces, as Richard, now beautifully dressed in their grandchildren's clothes, grinned at me. 'I was looking for Manda and Ouma.'

Preparations for the musical had gone well. All the sound and lighting equipment was in place, and worked. I had been to a number of Christian charity concerts where things had gone wrong. Microphones not switched on, electrical connections not made, slides upside down, movie film always snapping, smiling screeching singers, all were tolerated in the name of Christianity and, as we all knew, produced second-rate and more often third-rate theatre productions. 'Well, it's just a Christian production, you know. What can you expect?' I was determined that this would not be such a performance. As a result emotions were a little stretched as we had tried to bully the production into shape.

'Just do what he wants,' yelled the bass player at the sound man. 'If he says turn up the volume in the mid range, turn up the volume in the mid range. Stop faffing about.' Sound men would often grumble if you told them what you wanted. They were outstanding technicians, but some were not very musical. To get a good balance in those

41

early years was always a battle. There was an earthquake effect in the production which had to be loud. The sound man was unwilling to turn the volume up to the level I required because he thought it would break his speakers. It never did.

Word had got out that our church, already well known for unusual services, was going to put on this new musical. Almost an hour before the production started, the place was packed. We couldn't believe it. People streamed in from every door. They sat in the pews, on the floor and in the windows. The minister's wife smiled at me from behind the piano. She knew how nervous we all were.

'Look at all the people, Clive.' She winked. 'Isn't it wonderful?' It was amazing.

'Rob wants a word with you before we start, Clive.' It was one of the ushers, fighting through the crowd. 'He's next door.' I remember struggling towards the room we set aside for counselling, thinking that Rob, the service leader, after consultation with the minister, would want to run the presentation twice in order not to disappoint those people who might not get in to see the first performance. He was at a table together with the visiting preacher for the evening, a well-known national evangelist. I sat down.

'Clive, I've got to get up and introduce the evening in just a moment.' He looked at me unsmiling. 'I want to ask you, did you really write this thing?' I was surprised; I had been working on it for months, and he knew it. Now, moments before going in front of a large audience, I had a strange feeling that my integrity was about to be brought into question.

'You know I have. I've been working on it for ages.' Two pairs of eyes bored into me.

'It's just that Eric Royce came to see me a few moments

42

ago and told me that you didn't, that you stole it and that Chuck Girard wrote it.' I couldn't believe my ears.

'That's just not true,' I mumbled. I suppose I should have been flattered, as Chuck Girard is a well-known American Christian songwriter. I wasn't flattered. I believed that, at that moment, he thought I was lying to them.

'All right.' He nodded. He did not smile and did not wish me good luck, and all the while his guest remained silent. I stood up and walked across to where the choir and orchestra were waiting for me to lift and encourage them. I felt shattered.

You would be right in thinking that I felt unnecessarily aggrieved. After all, it was only a feeble musical effort – why should I feel so slighted by the question? The answer was simple. It *was* my effort. I *had* spent hours, days and months creating it. It had taken shape in *my* mind and I had poured something of myself into it. I had been reluctant to tell others that I had written it in case someone laughed; there is still a sort of schoolboy vulnerability about me. No one had laughed and now we were going to perform it. I suppose most writers feel this way about their creations and I was hurt. What really surprised me was that I just didn't expect it. It had never occurred to me, at that early stage of my new-found faith, that older, more mature Christians of stature and leadership could do such a thing: lie so easily.

'What's wrong, Clive?' asked Mike, the bass player. 'You don't look too good. Are you OK?'

'I'm OK,' I grinned weakly. 'Let's get on with it.'

The performance was a resounding success. Rob, the service leader, and the evangelist guest were full of public praise for the efforts of the team. But the matter was never mentioned again. We received several invitations to run the production in various parts of the city but not again in our own church. I have never written another musical since, and whenever I did write the occasional Christian song that friends would sing, I would not tell them where it came from. A great deal was explained to me intuitively that day – why equipment would disappear before crucial rehearsals, why microphones and amplifiers would find their way to 'other destinations' for the use of 'other song groups' and the choir would be left unable to rehearse fully. I never really recovered from the accusation that I had not written the music as, in my youthful Christian naivety, I believed that Christians helped each other and did not hinder them.

Some time later I found the courage to speak to Eric Royce because I wanted to know what it was that had caused him to make the accusation. He looked sympathetic but dismissed the incident with a wave of his hand, and said that he would never have said such a thing and that others had got it all confused and wrong. He promised to sort it out, but I don't suppose he ever did as the matter was never raised again. At the same time I knew that my own attitude needed to be dealt with. I also knew full well that I should not let something so silly get to me and that I should get on with life and use the talent, however limited, that God had given me. It's just that something died that Sunday evening. Something, I suppose, I was too scared to bring back to life. I have since discovered that similar things have happened to countless people in all walks of life on the receiving end of what is called 'professional jealousy'. It is something that most just have to roll with.

If we all gave into it, as I did, we would achieve nothing in this life for fear of ridicule.

I continued to be friendly to Eric and he continued as if nothing had happened. Forgiveness, I found that day, was a choice I had to make and not an emotion I had to feel. I had to forgive with my head and let my heart take care of itself. Later the hurt was replaced by some anger, but the passion of it was controlled. Now I was a Christian, I thought I was supposed always to feel kind and loving. Huh! I knew I had to forgive, but I didn't want to.

I had experienced double standards when dealing with businessmen of the world and was shocked to find that some Christians behaved no differently. I can remember one pastor from the United States telling me that when in conversation with one of his elders he had told him how much he valued his support as a friend.

'Don't you believe it,' the man said, 'you've got no friends in this place.' The next day a group of elders tried to oust the pastor from office. I was to find a chilling parallel in my own ministry some years later.

As I grew older and became more involved in church activities I began to meet more and more people who had to a greater or lesser degree been bruised, not so much by an unbelieving world but rather by those who were part of the same church. I found that in some circles, evangelicalism placed a larger portion of guilt upon its adherents than God ever does. For example, I was once berated by a clergyman for not attending a weekly Bible study. I had gone to watch an inter-provincial night series game of cricket. Then there was the occasional glass of wine at meal times. I was made to feel as if it were an unpardonable thing to enjoy such things now and then.

It began to strike me strongly that while evangelicalism was very good at bringing people to a personal faith it was not so good in taking them on from there. Often, in evangelical circles, a meeting's 'success or failure' was judged on the number of people who had come forward. I was beginning to be disturbed at how many converts had burnt out and fallen on the way, but the church leadership often seemed too busy to notice.

I put the incident of the musical behind me and got on with ministry. After all, there was more to this thing than my damaged pride. And in any event maybe I needed to be knocked off my little peg. At the end of the day I am certainly no Chuck Girard, or Andrew Lloyd Webber for that matter, and I suppose it is true to say that it was easy to fall into the trap of becoming over-involved. I really enjoyed supporting church work. It was fun and we had a lot of laughs, but there is always a fine dividing line between activity and growing in Christian maturity. I believe that I often got the two confused, especially in the area of drama and music.

5

A Leap of Faith

*Be strong and courageous. Do not be terrified; do
not be discouraged, for the LORD your God will be
with you wherever you go.*

(Josh. 1:9)

In the next few years I became involved in many more
activities. Apart from the music and drama I went to
counselling courses that were run by the church, I was
asked to lead the congregational singing on a Sunday and it
was only a matter of time before I got an invitation to attend
a meeting of the church council. I had no idea why.

'We've been watching you over the last year or so, Clive,'
the chairman said, 'and we believe that you should think
of going to college and then consider full-time ministry.'
I was bemused. This was the very last thing on my mind.
Of course, the proposal was out of the question. I was a
married man with three children; our youngest, Catherine,
born in January 1980, was only a few months old. I must
admit I was flattered, but the notion was sheer madness.
I left the meeting with very mixed feelings and some days
later I phoned the chairman, declined their suggestion and
put the matter out of my mind. I quite literally forgot all
about it until about six months later, when a NASA space

scientist and fellow Christian, Dr Herb Mitchell, who was also on the church council, suggested that I think the matter over as I had been the subject of a further discussion about becoming a minister.

'Herb, I just can't afford it, and I don't know if I really want to go.' Mary and I had begun talking about the prospect and although she was not against it, I was.

At this point, Paul Carter, an expatriate Brit who was just about to finish at theological college, was beginning to influence my thinking. Paul was an extremely likeable man and we got on very well. He had come through the swinging sixties set of wine, women and song as well as fast cars. He had been a sky-diving instructor before getting married to Sue, a hot-pants dancer from a go-go night club in Johannesburg. The two of them were the most unlikely ministerial material you could imagine. God must certainly have a sense of humour. But both of them were to become treasures in Christian ministry, Paul to lead several large churches and have a major role to play with the South African Broadcasting Corporation in both radio and television, and Sue to lead many women's retreats and seminars. Sadly I have since lost touch with them.

We were sitting around the swimming pool at my house when Paul quite bluntly said that he thought I should stop 'messing about' as he gently put it and 'get off my butt' and go to college. Paul is about the same height as me but about four stone heavier, and not much of that was fat. Well, not then at any rate. You don't argue much with Paul. We had been involved in drama and music at the church and had much in common. He had helped with the musical I had written, himself writing the narration. Of all the men that I knew, it is true to say that at the time he influenced me the most concerning going into the ministry.

'I don't know, Paul,' I said, sucking on the remains of a lamb chop – we had just had one of our famous *braais* (South African for barbecue) – 'my job is going really well and I'm enjoying what I'm doing right now.' I threw the bone to a slavering Tarus, who crunched it to pulp.

'If the Lord calls . . .' intoned Paul piously, and reached for a can of beer.

'Well,' I smiled as I stood up and moved to the edge of the pool, 'He had better shout a little louder,' and jumped into the cool water. But God was not going to shout any louder. What He was waiting for was for me to jump, not into the pool but into faith. Only at the time I didn't know that. What did happen took me as much by surprise as anyone else, and it came only a few weeks later.

It was early April 1982 and I went to work one morning, as usual. I was due to make a couple of calls on a large medical practice in the northern part of Cape Town together with a workmate who also happened to be a Christian and with whom I spent time on Monday mornings in prayer for our company and work colleagues. By the way, it is interesting to note that at the time we started praying, our sales increased and we became the top team in the country for a few years. I remember when we were asked for the secret of our success at a conference Lieb would say, 'Try prayer, and hard work.' The others thought we were joking, but we knew that we weren't.

Lieb and I had stopped in the surgery parking bay and were discussing strategy when I heard myself say, 'Lieb, I'm taking you back to the office. I'm going to resign.'

That was it. I almost couldn't believe that I had said it. Lieb's mouth fell open. I started the car, and before he could protest or I could change my mind we sped out of the car park and back to the office. The journey was spent in complete silence. Twenty minutes or so later I walked through the front door of my house.

'What's the matter?' asked Mary. 'Are you ill?'

'No,' I said, 'I've just resigned. We're going to Bible College.'

'Oh.' She looked at me, and then with typical calm and her unnerving ability to cope she simply said, 'Let's have a cup of tea.'

You may have the impression that I acted rashly and with little responsibility for a man with a mortgage, a wife and three children to care for. And to the outside world that is certainly how it would seem. Some of my friends called me irresponsible and accused me of ducking out of the real world to hide and cloister myself in the Church. Well, any clergyman will be quick to tell you that if you want to hide from reality then the Church is certainly not the place to do it. Mary and I had been discussing the prospect of full-time ministry at length; we had just not planned for it to come the way it did. But then God is full of surprises.

Many of those surprises were now to become more apparent. I had told Paul Carter that God should make his intentions a little more clear, when in fact what He wanted was a leap of faith. Now that I had taken that leap, would He be there to catch me? Judge for yourself.

A few days later, when word was out that I was

going to college, Dr Herb Mitchell came up to me at a church picnic.

'I believe you have made a decision, Clive.' He looked at me, his eyes sparkling.

'Yes Herb,' I replied, 'I don't know how I'm going –' The space scientist responsible for computer calculations that had sent the early Apollo moon missions into lunar orbit cut me short.

'Well, I'm paying for your fees and all your books for the next three years.' My jaw dropped open, just as Lieb's had done some time earlier. 'Here.' With extended thumb and index finger Herb placed a charcoal-encrusted sausage on my plate, grimaced and walked away.

In the Old Testament we read that when the Israelites had arrived at the River Jordan after forty years in the desert, Joshua told the priests who were carrying the ark to put their feet into the raging water. We are told that the river was in flood at the time. They could have said, 'Don't be daft, Josh, let's wait a few months until the river goes down. We've been walking for forty years, another few weeks won't make any difference.' The people could easily have camped beside the river and waited for the right time to cross. But a lack of faith in God would have robbed them of a miracle. In human terms, the priests took a very foolish step by risking the ark of God in the flood waters. But their feet had to be in the water before the miracle could take place.

Humanly speaking, I acted foolishly by giving up my secure job and going into the ministry. But from the moment I made the decision to go, things began to happen. I let my house for much more than my mortgage repayments. We found five-bedroomed accommodation almost next door to the college itself. My father-in-law offered to fly the entire family out to England for a holiday before we started studies. The children's education was all taken care of in a small school in Kalk Bay, where no fees were required for the children of theological students, and it was a place which was to turn Amanda around academically and ground her more firmly in her own studies. We would have a magnificent view across False Bay with a three-minute walk to the beach. And people said we acted foolishly. Well, it seems that God looks after fools. Especially if they are His fools. In all the years we spent studying, we were hardly ever in need of anything material. There was always enough food on the table, we could pay the rent, the children always had nice presents at Christmas and birthdays and I always had pocket money. You may smile at this, but I did not always have pocket money when I was working and drawing a salary. Not only was I now not drawing a salary, but Mary never had to work a single day to earn money while we were students. You can't explain that, apart from God's provision. We had stepped into the flood, and God had held the waters back. There is simply no other explanation.

Having said all this, I cannot say that being a theological student was the most spiritually exciting time in my life. In fact, it was for the most part a spiritually dry time. It was clinically academic: studies in the New Testament, studies in the Old Testament, studies in systematic theology, apologetics, hermeneutics, etc., etc., and, of course, Hellenistic Greek. All the while the choir I trained continued to grow and grow. Tuesday nights were the highlight of the week. I loved that choir and all its members and when I finally left it in 1987, to run my first church, it broke my heart.

I had studied at the University of Cape Town before I went to theological school but I would not regard myself as academic. I do not read easily. Partly because of my poor eyesight (but mostly because of inertia) I struggled to read as widely as I should have, especially in the 'years of study'. Naturally I have student memories, but these do not come to mind now. The events that stand out concern my son, Richard, and his contribution to my student life. He was about six years old when we moved to Kalk Bay and was always getting into mischief. He locked himself in a student toilet and it took the caretaker some hours to release the lock. He hid himself in the girls' boarding house so that he could spy on the ladies on their way to the bathroom; fortunately he was discovered, as six-year-olds are not very good at keeping quiet. On another occasion, he and I were walking through the grounds one early evening when one of the younger female students leant out of her window to greet me. Richard, who could whistle from an early age, did so and made a comment which one would not expect from one so young. I ushered him quickly from the smiling student and as we walked away I remember him putting his hand into mine, saying, 'She's quite pretty, eh Dad?'

'Nice one, Ricky,' I replied, 'you've got it made, son.' All this from a little boy who had let off a very, very loud burp as a minister was about to say grace before an evening meal.

But it was the day of the college photograph that I recall with most satisfaction. We had been given strict instructions on the dress code, as this was to be a formal event. Academic staff were to be suitably attired and it was all to be taken most seriously. One of the lecturers had received his PhD with a dissertation on the epistles of John. He sat stoically resplendent in his red robes. There were eighty or so students standing on the erected scaffolding, with the staff seated in chairs at the front. Several attempts to get it 'right' had resulted in some of the senior members of the faculty becoming somewhat crusty; they had little time for this frivolity. The assembled students were also getting a bit fidgety when through the gate, with his shirt-tails hanging, a satchel-dragging, blond-haired, blue-eyed boy appeared from behind the photographer and surveyed the scene before him. He had never seen the likes of it before and spotting his father in the back row he grinned.

'Hi, Dad,' he yelled at the top of his voice. 'Who's that funny guy in the front, Father Christmas or someone?' The doctor remained stoic, the students almost fell from the risers. I still have a copy of that picture. Every one of us is smiling. Every one.

6

A Prelude to Pain

Take care to sell your horse before he dies.
The art of life is passing losses on.

(Robert Frost)

I must have been ordained about two years when Richard was thrown out of a Sunday school class for misbehaviour. No doubt he had been tormenting some of his ten-year-old classmates. On one occasion he had been flung backwards through a swing door by a hefty lady Sunday school teacher when he had produced a dead frog from his pocket and offered it to her. This time it must have been a less offensive crime. He was outside the room contemplating his fortune when the pastor, who was making a rare visit to the Sunday school, found him sitting on the floor in the corridor.

'And why aren't you in your class, young man?' came the inevitable question.

Not wishing to be outdone and peering from underneath a wild mess of unkempt and very blond hair the boy retorted, 'And why aren't you in your pulpit?'

Only three days earlier I had dropped him off at school in the morning with instructions for him to wait for me after school, when I would pick him up. It had been a busy day counselling and preparing for the weekend services, and I finally got home at about five. My wife and two daughters greeted me as I arrived.

'Where's Richard?' Mary asked, expecting me to say that he was following. A sudden dread came over me.

'I forgot to collect him!' I FORGOT TO COLLECT HIM! I ran out to the car and raced up the street. The school wasn't too far away but it was rush hour and the traffic was heavy. I crawled along, angry and frustrated with myself. If only I hadn't been so preoccupied with my own activities. If only I spent more time with my own family instead of spending it with everyone else's. If only I had kept my promise with Richard to play tennis last Saturday. If only I wasn't so stupid. Why can't they go any faster? I was supposed to pick him up at two in the afternoon; now it was five fifteen. I turned into the school road. There was hardly any traffic now as I picked up speed and approached the locked school gates. There, sitting on his school case with his cap on his head, staring at every car that passed as he had been doing for over three hours, was my son. He stood up as the car came to a halt, opened the door and got in beside me.

'Richie,' I blurted, 'I'm so sorry I'm late.'

'Don't worry, Dad.' He looked at me with those piercing blue eyes, 'I knew you'd come.'

I knew you'd come. How those words burnt into my heart and little did I know how they would come to accuse and torture me about seven years later. We hotfooted it to the nearest ice-cream parlour where all was forgiven and forgotten in precious time spent laughing and talking about the day's events. He told me he had just been chosen to play inside centre in the school under-eleven rugby team. We were going to play our archrivals, Bishops, on Saturday.

A Prelude to Pain

This particular match stands out in my memory more than many he played. The reason is simple. The Bishops fly-half kicked off, the ball rose in the air and dropped into Richard's arms. He was beautifully proportioned and very well co-ordinated, albeit somewhat small for his age. He took off, chased by his team mates all yelling for him to pass the ball to someone else and everyone else. He didn't. He kept on running. Defenders fell like fallen logs. He was on Mercury's wings, and to the screams of delight from his team mates he dotted the ball down behind the posts – the quickest try scored that season. 'That's my boy,' I said to one cheering parent, 'That's *my* boy.'

Roger Page had come into my office earlier that week. It might have been on the day I had forgotten to pick Richard up. We had never met before, but his wife was a regular attender at our Sunday morning services and it was through her contact with me that he had decided to come and talk. He was in his late forties, about average height and slightly balding. He had the stature of a man who was used to authority and seemed confident in himself. I offered him a seat in an easy chair and sat down myself on a sofa which I had in my office. I disliked talking across a desk unless I had papers to deal with. I'm not sure if it was the relaxed informal atmosphere that prevailed or not, but immediately his eyes filled with tears. We had hardly exchanged greetings, let alone embarked upon a conversation. After an awkward pause he regained control.

'I've just lost my job,' he said, 'I don't know what to do.' Neither did I, so I kept my mouth shut. 'I've never been in this situation before and I'm not sure how I can provide for my family,' he continued. 'I don't know if you can help or even why I'm here. Caroline seems to think quite highly of you and –' he paused and looked at the ceiling, '– and I feel so bloody silly about these tears.' He fumbled for the hankie he didn't have.

'That's OK,' I said as I got up and moved towards my desk. 'It sometimes goes with the territory.' I pulled open a drawer and took out a tissue box. It was empty. I couldn't believe it. I must have looked rather odd because Roger burst out laughing. I looked at him over the top of my half-specs and grinned sheepishly. In that moment I knew we would get on just fine.

The story that followed was one of betrayal. I know it was only his side of the story, and I've no doubt it was a weighted story, but I believed the essence of it completely.

Roger had been a director of a very large clothing corporation in Cape Town. He was one of the senior men and answered only to the chairman of the group. On a day-to-day basis it would have been almost impossible to get an appointment with him in his office unless you had made it well in advance or you were a very senior man in your own field. His annual salary would have run into six figures. He was powerful, successful and highly qualified. His house was paid for and he had no debts. His children, still in their teens, were at good schools. He was well fixed in the 'things of this world'. But now he was unemployed and the prospects of his finding similar work were slim. In short he was, to use his own term, 'overqualified'. Don't you just love that word?

He had gone to work one morning as usual. Everything seemed normal until he arrived at his office. His secretary was not at her desk, which was strange, and at his own was the chairman of the board. The chairman began by asking Roger how he felt about moving back to head office in Johannesburg. Roger did not relish the prospect at all unless it were to secure a more senior post. It was not, and was clearly a sideways move. It would take a very brave man to move to Johannesburg from Cape Town if there were nothing in it for himself; those with any sense were making the opposite journey. Cape Town was then and certainly is now a much better prospect for those who want family security, a better culture and much better spiritual values, let alone scenic beauty. Crime in South Africa, since full democracy and the end of white rule, has increased dramatically, not least in Cape Town but especially in Johannesburg. Mugging, murder, rape, car hijacking and house-breaking are the order of the day unless one is prepared to live behind a barrier of barbed wire and electronically controlled gates and doors. One would have to be courageous – even foolish – to want to live in Johannesburg. Roger was not a foolish man.

'I don't think it's what I or my family want right now, David,' he said to the chairman, 'We are on top of things here. We have the highest production quota in the country and, what's more, we are 15 per cent over projected forecasts. The children are settled at school and Katie has only one more year to go before she finishes. If only for this reason I would not want to move her at this stage.' But as he spoke Roger knew something was about to change. It was the chairman's mood.

'You don't have a choice. I and my family want to move to Cape Town, so you will have to move to head office. Peter Simes will be your immediate superior.'

As Roger recounted the story I sensed his growing anger

and frustration. The tears he had shed a few moments ago were not those of self-pity but of controlled rage. He spoke more quickly as the saga unfolded. Here was a man who had been asked to sacrifice the security of his family for the selfish desire of another man and his wife. It was a move which made no economic sense at all and might well have proved disastrous for the company. But he was powerless, and that sense of powerlessness had increased the frustration he felt.

'What did you say?' I asked, almost breathless from the tragedy of it.

'Nothing at first, but I had the strongest desire to attack him. To beat his stupid face in.' He clapped his fist into an open palm. 'At that moment I wanted to really hurt him.' Roger stared at the fish tank on my bookshelf. 'But it was when he told me that I had no choice that it sort of clicked over for me. We always have a choice, Clive – we might have to take the consequences of that choice, but we always have a choice. I could have chosen to capitulate and do whatever he said or I could have chosen to refuse and then take what came. Let no man tell you that you don't have a choice.' Roger looked at me for a moment as if he were playing with the tension. 'Then I told him to stick his job right up his fat arse. Sorry, Clive,' he said as he remembered my office.

'That's OK, Roger,' I grinned. 'It gets hotter than that in here sometimes.'

'I picked up my briefcase and walked out,' he continued. He seemed calmer now. 'I had joined the group on my twenty-second birthday, just after I graduated from university. Twenty-seven years of service.' He shook his head. 'Twenty-seven years! Do you know what I'm doing with my

time at the moment?' I shook my head. 'I'm working on the
tugboats down at the docks.'

'The what?' I shook my head again. 'Tugboats?'

'Yup, I'm a stevedore. It's all I can find at the moment.
Nobody wants to employ me in the trade I know and if I
don't fill my day with some activity, I'll go crazy. So I do
manual labour. It's a killer on the hands and back, but it
keeps my mind off things for the moment.'

'How are your family taking all this?' I asked.

'Caroline is OK. She has a much stronger faith in God
than I do. She has got herself a job as a receptionist and
it pays for the food. I've been paid out my pension but
I need to re-invest that. The girls are a bit upset, mainly
because we have had to let some things go, the car for one,
but I think we are closer as a family. We certainly spend
more time together. And although I'm mad, really angry
at what has happened, I don't shout at them as much as
I used to.'

I looked at Roger as he sat relating his story. He was
luckier than most in his position. He did have a home that
was paid for and he did have a supportive family. He had
resources at his disposal and he still had good health. He
would recover in time and the circumstances would lead
him closer to God. It was just that at that moment he
could not see it. Maybe he didn't want even to hear it.
Not now.

'I have this overpowering sense of wanting revenge, Clive.'
I was half-surprised at the statement because he did not
seem like a vengeful man. However, I could understand
his desire for a pound of flesh. 'How do I deal with it?'
This is the moment pastors are supposed to have all the
answers. I could not relate to Roger's situation. I had not

experienced anything like it in my life. Not at that time. A few years later it would be a different story, but for now I was expected to pass judgment on it. 'I want to hurt them as much as they have hurt me. All I ever did for them was in their interests. I worked hard for them. I feel gutted and betrayed and I have to drag my family along for the ride.'

'First you can thank God for your family. Second, you don't want to make it any more difficult for them, so although you may not like it you have to let it go. It's out of your hands. You will only do more harm to yourself and to them by allowing this emotion to take control.'

'But that's just it,' he interrupted. 'I can't do anything about the emotion. It's there. I feel it. It won't go away.'

'You're right about it being there,' I said. 'It's real and raw and it hurts and you can't do anything about the feelings, but you can do a great deal with what you do with those feelings.' He looked at me, confused. I wasn't surprised because I was a bit confused myself. 'What I mean is this: while the emotion is strong, you don't have to put it into action. You don't have to beat his head in. You don't have to bad-mouth the firm to others. It's a choice you can make. You said it yourself about choices. You can walk away from it and take the feelings with you. In time they will diminish.'

'But I'm not sure I want to walk meekly away.' Roger folded his arms defensively across his chest.

'Then your passion will, in the end, consume you. They will have more than your job, they'll have your life as well. Let it go, Roger.' He had come into my office to see me in my capacity as a Christian pastor and it was only fair to let him know what my yardstick for measuring

the situation would be. If he had gone to a psychologist
or secular counsellor he would have had to accept their
principles. 'God takes vengeance in His own way and in
His own time,' I continued, as I reached for the Bible on
my desk. 'The Scripture is emphatic about this.' I quoted
from Paul's letter to the Romans (12:19), Deuteronomy
(32:35), the Psalms (94:1) and Hebrews (10:30). 'You see,'
I said as I put the book down, 'if you want to destroy
your enemy you have to make him your friend.'

Roger laughed and looked away. 'My friend!' he said
ruefully. 'Don't be pathetic. I don't want to be walked
all over.'

'The Christian ethic cuts right across what comes naturally to us,' I said. 'We feel meekness is weakness. It isn't.
The only way you can walk away from all this is if you
make a determined effort to do so.'

Roger looked at his hands and rubbed his thumb into
his palm. We had been talking for almost two hours. I
remember thinking how fortunate I was to be employed
by the Church. Why was it that most secular companies
could not behave like church people? This sort of treachery
would never happen to a minister. 'Well, I'll go away and
think about it all.' He began to rise and sat again as I held
up my hand.

'Can we pray for a moment?'

Roger started to come to church on a regular basis and
even joined a men's support group. He went away on one
or two men's retreats and made a sincere commitment to
Christianity. Some time later he secured a good post in
another part of the country and we lost contact. But in the
years to come I was to remember Roger and my advice to
him, advice I found very difficult to accept and follow even

if it was my own. It was as if I were unknowingly glimpsing the future and watching my own prelude to pain.

I have come across a number of cases like Roger's where people have been betrayed in the workplace or betrayed in the bedroom. The hurt is all-embracing. People suffer all manner of debilitating physical conditions as a result of the stress: insomnia, weight loss, back pain, ulcers. Some even have skin irritation or suffer from eating disorders. The list is never-ending. There is no quick fix, no easy answer. Some can bounce back from it a lot better than others. Some just cannot find relief from the burden of betrayal. I have found, however, that those with a stronger spiritual base are more likely to have a better resource to deal with the crisis. They are not immune – many Christians have suffered terribly – but it is true that most would not have coped as well without that foundation of faith.

7

The Other Side of the Valley

*The wind of change is blowing through this continent,
and whether we like it or not, this growth of national
consciousness is a political fact.*

(Harold Macmillan)

In 1988 Mary and I, together with our son and two
daughters, had moved from Cape Town to Hillcrest in
Natal. It was an affluent, middle-class town not far from
Durban and for us this was a time of great blessing and
growth. Not too far from all the luxury and comfort of
Hillcrest lay the sprawling terrain of what is called the
Valley of a Thousand Hills. It is aptly named. However,
behind the idyllic imagery of the beautiful setting lay quite
a different picture.

Hundreds of thousands of Zulu people lived, for the
most part, in mud huts and unhygienic conditions. Many
found shelter beneath black plastic sheeting draped over
thorn bushes. Some, more fortunate than others, made their
homes in large concrete sewerage pipes, abandoned by the
Natal provincial council working on reduced budgets. It
was a cauldron of humanity, with bread and maize as the
staple food and alcohol and drugs as the main source of
relaxation. Crime and violence were a way of life. And all

this was exacerbated by the ongoing political tensions that were rife in the late 1980s and early 1990s.

Samuel was our church's on-site, live-in gardener-cum-tea-boy and security officer. He was a noble and proud Zulu, in the ancient tradition. Employed by the church full time, he earned very little, as did most like him. Labour was, after all, cheap and plentiful. In fact many would vie for low wages simply to get a job. In a sense, they were a people betrayed.

Crushed by the colonial power of Queen Victoria's red-coated dragoons, exploited by the white settlers who followed and finally brought to heel by the shackles of Afrikaner apartheid, these people were indeed bowed low. Samuel would never greet you unless you first greeted him; you could see the sign of submission in the eyes of all the people of this proud nation. For the Zulu are more than a black African tribe – much more. They are a nation indeed.

Zulu is the name that is now given to the many sub-groups of the Nguni people who were forged into a single, powerful and coherent society under their great nineteenth-century leader, Shaka, a brilliant, fierce and ruthless military strategist who was known for executing his *impi* (warriors) with the very spear that they had chanced to drop.

The Zulu homeland is KwaZulu and is mother-earth to eight million people: the largest ethnic bloc in southern Africa. They are the most powerful and warlike of all the nineteenth-century nations. Their history is proud and their cultural traditions strong. Sadly, these traditions are being eroded by Western influences, as the once feared warrior is now costumed only for the benefit of the tourist.

The scenery in KwaZulu is spectacular. The foothills of the mighty Drakensberg Mountains are a natural paradise of grassy slopes and deep valleys, presided over by the Giant's Castle where fauna and flora abound.

'What's the matter, Samuel?' I enquired as I found him scowling in the kitchen. He threw the tea-towel aside and walked to his *kiya* (little hut). I looked at Rosemary, my secretary, and raised my eyebrows.

'Trouble at home,' she said. 'He has just found out that his wife has had a child, and it is not his.' I drew in my breath and returned to my office. A few moments later, muffled voices drew me from the theology of our Lord's Sermon on the Mount to a heated discussion taking place in the outer office. It was in very quick Zulu and I couldn't even get the gist of it. I opened the door.

'He wants to go home,' said Rosemary, who spoke Samuel's language fluently. 'He wants to go home and kill his wife, her boyfriend and the baby.' Samuel was standing by the desk, ashen and shaking with rage. 'If they were here now, I believe he would do it.' Rosemary was staring at me.

'Samuel . . .'

'Master,' he interrupted, the muscles in his face twitching, 'Master must just keep quiet.' His tone was measured and threatening. I had never seen him like this before. I held his gaze.

'I will try to organise you some transport, Samuel. But it may take a day or so.' I lied to that troubled Zulu man that day, and I take no pleasure in admitting it. But I had to play for time. I needed to keep him on site for a couple of days in the hope that his rage would subside. If he believed that I could arrange some transport for him he would wait for it; otherwise it would have taken him many days or even weeks to travel the several hundred kilometres to his home. If he had started out that morning, the passion of his anger would have grown with each step. I had to keep him from taking the first one. 'So will you please make us all some tea.'

Samuel always made the tea. He made it several times a day. I suppose it was his excuse to get out of the garden when the weather was too warm. He would sometimes bring me three or four cups in the morning. He turned stoically towards the kitchen. His offering was appalling – in fact, it was not fit for human consumption. Rosemary sent him off on another errand and the liquid was consigned to the sink.

A week or so later, the 'transport' had still not material-ised, but Samuel's smiles had. Even the tea had improved. A visit from one of his children had told him that it was not his wife who had produced a child, but his fourth daughter. He was now a grandfather – again. He spent much of the week celebrating in his room with a bottle and his live-in girlfriend.

A month later I had a very different encounter with a much younger Zulu man.

It was about three in the morning when the telephone rang. It was the security company which controlled our burglar alarm at the church. It had been activated and as a key-holder I was alerted and asked to meet the police at the building, three or four minutes' drive away from my house. After phoning one of the church elders and asking him to accompany me, I phoned another sleepy voiced member of the congregation and asked him to come to my house and await my return. Mary was away at the time and I did not relish the prospect of leaving the children alone; it was possible that the alarm had been set off to get me out of the house and thus leave it unprotected. Within minutes my sleepy friend arrived, suitably armed. I made my way to the church to be met by flashing blue lights.

'There has been one break-in over there,' shouted an officer over the wailing siren and pointed to the main church door which stood wide open, 'and one window in the office block has been smashed.' I turned the key in the alarm lock and a merciful peace settled over the valley again. Police torches stabbed the blackness.

'No one inside the building here,' said one as he emerged on to the lawns. 'Would you unlock the office, please.' I did so and slid back the security gate.

'This is my secretary's office,' I motioned. 'Nothing has been disturbed here, and through here is my office.' I snapped on the lights. A strong hand grabbed me from behind and pulled me back.

'Get out!' commanded the security man, 'Get out, there is someone in your office.' I was roughly pushed on to the lawn as he and his two colleagues, revolvers drawn, charged into the room. The sound of scuffling, shouting, swearing and punching followed. It seemed to go on and on. I remember thinking to myself, 'I wish they would stop – surely they have apprehended the intruder.' Finally the three grown men emerged, dragging the half-dead form of a young Zulu teenager. He had been badly beaten and was bleeding profusely. I was shaking and felt sickened; I had to look away. One of the men came up to me with a machete in his hand.

'If you had gone in, sir, he would have cracked your skull open.' I was speechless. 'If not now, then when you

69

opened up in the morning. You see, he'd got in by squeezing through the burglar bars, but he couldn't get out. He was under the desk waiting for the morning.' I stared at the battered boy now being unceremoniously dumped in the back of the truck. 'If we had just re-set the alarm and gone off without checking the office, then the first one through the door in the morning would be dead,' the officer said, slamming the door. 'Oh, good God,' I thought. Rosemary was often the first at the office.

'What will happen to him?' I motioned towards the police van.

'We will clean him up, put a few stitches in him and in a few days they'll let him out. There is no room for them any more. Jails are just bloody full.' He turned towards the van. 'Sorry about the mess inside, but I don't think we broke anything.' 'I don't think we broke anything!' A later inspection would show two blood-splattered offices, but nothing was broken. No, nothing was broken.

I returned home to relieve the guardian of my children. 'Thanks, Wes,' I said. He looked at me gravely.

'There were some prowlers in the garden, but when the dogs barked and they saw me moving about, they took off. Are you all right?'

I shook my head. 'Go home to your family. I'll tell you tomorrow.'

'You mean today,' he grinned as he opened his car door.

'Oh, Wes,' I called as he climbed into his seat, 'don't tell Mary about the prowlers. They may not have been related to the break-in'. He nodded and drove away.

A few weeks later, a decisive change took place in South Africa. After an illness the Prime Minister, P.W. Botha, was forced out of office and F.W. de Klerk was chosen by the ruling Nationalist Party to take charge. Many in the country felt a sense of gloom: it was well known that de Klerk was not in favour of sharing power with the Blacks. I was convinced that the violence, already widespread, would intensify. But it was as though fate was to take over. Suddenly change began to occur at almost breathtaking speed as de Klerk set in motion a series of events that would lead to the end of apartheid.

I was astonished at the change of direction that de Klerk took. It was as if the Prime Minister had a death wish about him, not for his country but for his Afrikanerhood. It was a complete turnabout in everything his fathers had stood for, in separateness. Whether he actually wanted it or whether he could do nothing but watch we will never really know, but I clearly remember watching the television late in the afternoon of 11th February 1990, and seeing the fruits of his efforts: a tall, grey-haired black man walking away from a prison gate on the outskirts of Cape Town after twenty-seven years. It was incredible – literally too hard to believe. For forty-two years the country had followed a policy of keeping people of different races apart. Now, with the stroke of the jailer's pen, it had ended with this man walking into the sunlight and into history.

'What do you think, Dad?' Richard was standing at my shoulder.

'Well, Rick,' I said, 'it had to be, but how it will all end only time will tell. But the Zulus won't be all that thrilled.' I looked over my shoulder and suddenly jumped out of my seat. 'What's that? What have you got in your hands?'

'It's a fish.'

'I can see that, I'm not blind! It's dripping on the carpet – get it out of here, your mother will have a fit.'

'I just caught it with Don at the lake.' He beamed. 'Pretty good, hey?'

'GET IT OUT.'

'OK, OK, just don't ask for some of it later.' My son sauntered off to the kitchen with his two-foot prize as I frantically mopped the carpet with a tea-towel, now oblivious to the flickering pictures on the television screen behind me.

'Hot wind,' Samuel informed me the next day as he placed another cup of tea on my desk. 'Hot wind.'

'What on earth do you mean, Samuel?' I had never thought of Samuel as being politically informed.

'Mandela,' he said. 'He will be good for you white people and his Xhosas, he wants to keep you, but us Zulus –' he paused as Lucy, our cleaner, entered the room and they exchanged a few comments in Zulu, '– us Zulus and the others . . .' He drove his fist into his palm and shook his head. By 'others' Samuel was referring to the so-called Asian and coloured citizens of South Africa.

'Samuel, it had to be. I think that he will appeal to all South Africans, white and black. The whole world was against the government. It wasn't right. He had to be set free.'

'What do you know about right? You don't sleep in the valley.' Lucy waved her duster at me. This was uncharacteristic of her and her voice was disapproving. 'You don't hear the cries of the children when the ANC gunmen come and shoot their fathers. Last night I slept in the bushes because they were burning the houses again.' She rubbed the coffee table furiously with her cloth. 'Mandela

72

and that wife of his, they are not Zulu.' I could not believe my ears. I had honestly believed that all Blacks had welcomed Nelson Mandela's release. I was wrong.

'Clive, we have got to do something about it. Please come and see for yourself.' Noel Wright, my rector's warden, spoke softly over the phone. 'I'll pick you up in half an hour and we can drive out there.' 'Out there' was an hour's drive to an old abandoned farmhouse which was now part of a school for black children. The sight which greeted us was one of unbelievable squalor. Some five hundred children were crammed into one house for the purpose of being educated. There were no books, no blackboards. Some old single desks which had no tops were used by three or four pupils. Most sat on the mud floors. Toilets were blocked and foul-smelling as the water had been turned off. The senior teacher shook his head sadly.

'They've forgotten about us. Neither the ANC, nor Inkatha, nor the government will give us any money because we fall into an area that is not controlled by any of them. We turn off the water because the *skebenga* [thieves] steal the taps to sell for wine.' Worse was to follow as he led us up some alarmingly rotten wooden stairs which groaned under our weight. The boards which supported the upper floors and a further two hundred children were almost non-existent. Gaping holes allowed us to peer down on to the classrooms beneath.

'What can we do?' asked Noel in a state of shock.

'Just get us some books.'

'Paint? Wood? Tools?' I blurted like a fool.

'No, some of the parents will just come in the night and steal them. Just some books. Please.'

73

Noel and I, together with the headmaster of a local white junior school, began to amass old discarded books. We got them from anywhere and everywhere. We even received a shipment of old biology books from the United States. Some were totally irrelevant. Some were even in strange languages. But our black schoolmaster received them all with much clapping and singing. What he later said to me has burned itself into my mind as deeply as the pictures of the children sitting silently in their broken school among their broken furniture, with what amounted to not much more than their broken dreams.

'They can take away our taps. They can take away our paint and our wood. They can take the clothes from our backs and the shoes from our feet, but they cannot take away what we learn. They cannot take away our education.'

I do not cry easily, but at that moment I walked away from that man as he stood with his arm around a little black schoolgirl who was clutching a book written in English – a book she could not even read – and stood on the dust bowl of their football pitch and fought back the tears. Most of it was shame and self-pity. How fortunate I had been in my youth. How blessed were my children, and yet how wretched I was for not doing more for these people.

My ministry in Natal was one of the most precious times that Mary, the family and I enjoyed. We loved the little congregation dearly and they reciprocated in so many ways. Why we ever left it remains a mystery to me even to this day – it was probably the biggest mistake of my life to leave those dear people and move back to Cape Town. A fateful decision. One clergyman of many years' standing said to me, 'Clive, you are a fool. You are moving from butter to margarine.' He was wrong; it would be worse than that.

74

8

Kitchen Knives and Bulldogs

Is this a dagger which I see before me?
                    (William Shakespeare)

Therefore never send to know for whom the bell tolls; It tolls for thee.
                    (John Donne)

Ministry is often wide and varied. Pastors are called on to deal with all walks of life and all sorts of situations. Most ministers would be able to fill volumes with anecdotes of events that happen in their ministry – human stories of hope and despair, triumph and tragedy, laughter and tears. Often these can be uncomfortably close bedfellows. For example, one afternoon, in the space of one hour, I conducted a funeral of heart-rending sadness in a bleak, cold, red-brick crematorium attended by less than half a dozen frozen, sunken-eyed octogenarians, and then moved straight into a wedding rehearsal with a bubbling, bright-eyed bride-to-be and her handsome prince, complete with the bridesmaids, the best man and groomsman, the giggly flower girls and boisterous pageboy, the proud parents and the triumphant strains gushing from the organ pipes. How would it have

75

seemed to them if I had carried the melancholy of fifteen minutes past into this flower-bedecked auditorium?

Most ministers' memories would indeed be able to fill volumes. My ministry was little different and a few such events stand out in my mind.

The warm summer had dragged on and the days were long and golden. One cool evening at about six the telephone rang. It was John Clarke, one of the men responsible for counselling in the church.

'Clive, we have a problem and I'm hoping you can help me.'

'What is it, John?' I asked, as I sipped on the long ice-cold Coke I had just poured. I certainly was not prepared for what was to follow.

'A family in the northern suburbs are having a problem. A woman has locked herself in a neighbour's garage because her husband has been after her with a gun. The police have been called and . . .'

'What?' I could not believe what I was hearing. 'You want *me* to go into that sort of situation? What on earth do you think I can do to help?'

'Clive, she comes to our church and you are the nearest to her. Don't be such a coward. As I've just said, the police have been called and have probably arrested the guy by now. In any event, you know how to handle these situations.'

'Do I? Well, that's a comfort. Give me the address.' I sighed into the mouthpiece and scribbled directions. Replacing the receiver I took another swallow of Coke and began to make a great show of looking for my car keys, which I knew full well were beside my bed. On an impulse I picked up the phone again and called Alex Christopher, a huge Englishman who lived a few doors away and who had recently become a Christian. He was now attending services at our church and seemed keen to get involved.

'Alex,' I said, 'I'd like you to come with me to a family about ten minutes away. I think you will benefit from the experience. Can I pick you up in two minutes? There might be a problem as I believe that there is a weapon involved.'

'What's the problem, Clive?' asked Alex a short while later as he manoeuvred his six-foot-six, eighteen-stone frame into the car, his head, as always, touching the roof.

'Well, I don't know any details as yet,' I said as I looked over my shoulder to reverse out of his drive, 'but it seems that there's this chap that's been somewhat hard on his wife, and John had just got a call about it.' I moved the car forward down the road. 'Because I'm closest to them geographically, he thought I should go. I then thought it would be good for you to tag along . . .' Why is it that when ministers don't like doing something themselves they often find some other underling and suggest to them that the task they want them to perform is of monumental importance and would be 'a good experience' for them? If I were to be honest, it was not for Alex's benefit that I had asked him to come, it was for mine. Surely, if the man in question had not yet been apprehended by the police, then I would have adequate protection from the huge Alex Christopher.

The journey was all too short. As bad luck would have it, no traffic lights barred our path. There were no road works to make the route difficult, no overturned trucks to thwart us. In fact the directions that I had been given to lead us to our destination were all too perfect. We arrived in about fifteen minutes.

It was a working-class suburb and the terraced houses were quite run down. Grass grew out of the pavements and weeds grew in the tiny gardens. There was a rusty iron gate to number 47 and one hinge had come right out of the red-brick wall. An old car stood on wooden blocks in the street. Its wheels had been removed and oil seeped into the gutter. A pair of bare feet stuck out from underneath the front bumper. As Alex and I moved towards the gate there was a clunk, a bonk and the sound of a spanner falling to the ground. This was followed quickly by a rude word from beneath the car. We pushed at the gate and walked up the path. Suddenly the front door of the house flew open, and there stood a little man of about fifty-five, no more than five foot five and weighing about nine stone. He was dressed in a pair of shorts, from which protruded two spindly legs, and a threadbare vest which partially concealed the tattoo of a naked woman on his chest. He was unshaven and was clearly very drunk. You can have no illusions about his language which I shall describe thus: '$%ˆ&*'

'So,' he bellowed, 'you've $%ˆ&* come to $%ˆ&* interfere (hic) in my $%ˆ&* life. Go on and $%ˆ&*, the lot of you (hic).' Huge Alex rounded on the man.

'You've been drinking, mate. Don't talk like that to a minister. 'He's come to help you.'

'$%ˆ&*'

At that a haggard woman appeared at the door. She looked desperate, her eyes pleading. She motioned to us and ushered us in to a filthy sitting-room. The stale smell of sweat, mingled with old beer and tobacco, filled the room. Empty beer bottles littered the floor.

'Where's the gun?' I asked her. 'I was told that you were locked in a garage!' She looked at me strangely.

Isn't it amazing how messages can get so completely muddled up?

'There's no gun,' she said, 'but Barney, that's him,' she nodded towards the door, 'he's been drinking for nearly two weeks solid. We just can't take it any more. So I phoned someone at the church and asked them for help. I don't know anything about a gun.'

'I was told that the police had been called and that your husband was going to shoot you.'

'No,' she said, shaking her head, 'he's just been beating on us, but he's too drunk to do any real harm.' She paused as her husband, who had just finished swearing at the young man working on his car in the street, came into the room. 'Can you talk some sense into him, please?'

For the next hour and a half I did no talking. None. Barney did it all, with his face at all times not more than six inches away from mine. I had to turn my head away to breathe; the smell from his mouth was overpowering. As I moved away from him, so he kept moving closer. At one time I thought I would pass out from the stench of it all. At times a shower of spittle would land on my face. All his hatred of life was being poured out on to me: how he had been unfairly treated at work, how his brother had cheated him out of some money, how much he hated God and anything to do with the church. On and on it went. Whenever there was the slightest pause I tried to get a word in. All was to no avail and his ranting would take on new zeal.

Quite reasonably, one may wonder why I stood it for six minutes, let alone more than sixty. To this day I do not know the answer to that question, but I did recognise that here was a man distressed, if not possessed. I felt sorry for

79

him but I knew that there was no way I could get through to him unless he calmed down or there was some sort of divine intervention. There was neither. Suddenly he sprang towards the door.

'Do you want to see something?' he was shouting, spray flying. 'Do you $%^&* want to see something? Hey?' I was somewhat relieved at not having him so close.

'Yes, er, OK,' I said. He staggered from the room. The sound of crashing cutlery from the kitchen followed.

'Oh God!' His wife put her hand to her mouth. I felt myself tensing and looked at Alex. We stood still in the centre of the room. Barney almost fell through the doorway.

'I'll $%^&* show you something.' In his right hand was an enormous carving knife. I remember that it had an ivory handle and a blade of at least twelve inches. He raised his left wrist at arm's length in front of him and drew the knife behind his right shoulder as if to slash down on himself. I was aghast. My heart was pounding in my mouth. Nothing had prepared me for this. Six-foot-six and eighteen-stone Alex had now leapt behind me, his eyes wide with terror. There was nothing between me and this madman. Suddenly, out of nowhere a pretty teenage girl appeared from behind her drunken father. She grabbed his wrist.

I do not know if he ever intended to slash himself, or if he wanted to attack me, or if the whole episode was just a big show. I suppose I will never know the answer to that question. What I do know is that the situation certainly and suddenly became very grave as father and daughter flailed about. Even if it was now a drunken accident, that sweeping carving knife could have done real damage to himself or his little girl. I moved in quickly. It was not courage or bravado, neither was it fear. It seemed to be instinct. In a flash I had overpowered the little man, removed his weapon and flung it into a corner as if it were a viper. Now I was mad. I was furious. I like to think of myself as usually a mild-tempered man, but not then. I pushed Barney into a chair and let him have it, verbally. My adrenalin levels must have been way over the top. I shook him and yelled at him. My passive approach was gone. Gone? It had fled, fled from the fear of my raw anger which was just under control. I told him what he had done to himself, to his wife, to his children and to me. I told him that I was about to plant my fist so far down his throat that I would pull his backside out through his teeth. Do you know, I think he believed me. All of a sudden he went quiet and stared at me, transfixed by my every word. His eyes cleared in an instant as if he were stone cold sober.

'And now you are going to bed.' I picked him up like a child and carried him to his bedroom. His wife had pulled back the sheets and I laid him down on them. Instantly he was asleep. We pulled the blankets over him and left the room. I turned to his startled family. 'Call your doctor and ask him to come and give him an injection now as he may vomit in his sleep. You can tell the doctor exactly what has happened. Here is my phone number if you need me.'

Alex and I sat for a few silent moments in my car. 'Er, Alex,' I said as we both stared ahead into the darkened street, 'if ever you get yourself into that sort of situation, I would not advise you use my example of counselling language. No, it was not appropriate.' I started the car. We travelled home in almost complete silence. Every traffic light was against us. We took a wrong turn and it took an extra thirty minutes before we arrived at his house.

'Fancy a beer, mate?' For the first time since I had arrived at Barney's house some two hours earlier, our eyes met. We climbed out of the car together.

The following night at about eight o'clock the telephone rang. It was Barney's wife. He was drunk and violent and would I please come and put him to bed again. It was Mary who took the call. Wisely she suggested that the police be called and a charge of common assault be made. (Why didn't I think of something like that?) That way Barney could be taken into custody and given the opportunity to sober up. I never heard from them again. I did see him at church once some time later, clean-shaven and tidy, but he avoided my eyes and didn't speak to me.

I mentioned earlier a funeral that had pulled on my heart strings. It was the funeral of a man who had been full of years. Funerals are never easy; even triumphant Christian funerals are tinged with tears. But it is the burial of children that rips through the pastor's heart. Everyone else is allowed their tears, but if he weeps then it sweeps through a congregation like a crashing waterfall. I have not often dealt with the death of children; after all, we expect to bury our parents, not our babies. I received a call that a family I did not know well had lost their five-year-old son during a surgical operation.

They had been faced with an impossible dilemma. Their little boy had to undergo this procedure or his life expectancy would be about a year. They were also told that the operation itself was not without risk. In fact the risk was great. A nightmare scenario. They could take no action and watch their beloved child slowly get weaker until death came in about a year, or proceed with an operation that might be successful but, equally, might end the child's life within twenty-four hours. In anguish, they chose the operation and tragically he did not survive it.

I called on the devastated family. After the first few days of prayer and counselling, the funeral had to be planned.

'I know it is so hard now that Timothy is gone,' his mother said as we sat in the garden of their home drinking tea, 'but as there will be so many children who will be coming from his play school we had hoped that you could make the service meaningful for them.' I sipped from a mug as I watched Timothy's elder sister playing with her mother's hair. Timothy's father hardly spoke during this time of sadness and whenever he did he would end up in tears; it was Timothy's mother who seemed the stronger. How do you make the funeral of a child meaningful to children? I didn't have a clue.

'O God,' I prayed later in the day as I sat at my desk with my head in my hands, 'what do I say? What do I do? *What do I do?*' Pausing in my prayer, I rubbed the back of my neck and stared at the two goldfish swimming around and around the fish tank in my office. Beside the tank lay the lead and leather collar that belonged to our bulldog Emily. I looked at the fish and then at the collar. The fish . . . the collar. The fish . . . I reached for the Bible on my desk and turned to the passage most read at funerals, 1 Corinthians 15:35, 'The Resurrection Body'. 'How are the dead raised? With what kind of body will they come? . . . All flesh is not the same. Men have one kind of flesh, animals have another, birds another and fish another . . .' Suddenly I knew what I would do. It was not my own idea. I believe that at that moment God put the thought right into my mind. You may think whatever you like, but

I was not bright enough to think such a thought on my own. I needed my teenage son, Richard, to help.

'You are nuts, Dad. I always thought so, but now I know. OK, I'll help. I'll look after Adam.' Richard grinned at me later that evening and ran his fingers through the blond mop that grew out of his skull. 'Nuts!' He walked away, shaking his head.

There were over three hundred people at Timothy's funeral service. Sixty or seventy were children, all under the age of ten. The church was packed to the doors. Many were not Christians. How would they respond to my somewhat unorthodox approach? We would soon find out. I stared at the tiny white casket at the front of the church and steeled myself.

After preliminary greetings and the opening hymn I spoke to the congregation. My voice was strong and steady. I do not know how I found the strength to do it; it could only have come from God Himself. Believe me, I felt totally inadequate.

'I'd like all you children to come here and sit down with Timothy and me.' I placed my hand on the little coffin. They did not need a second invitation. They poured from their seats. The coffin did not faze them in the slightest and they were perfectly behaved. Sitting around their little dead friend they stared at me with eyes alight and full of life. I felt my throat tighten, and swallowed.

'Well, we all know why we are here,' I began. It sounded hollow. Many of the adults were moved by the sight of so many children sitting around a tiny coffin. I had to try and speak to their hearts as well. 'We have come to say goodbye to Timothy because he was sick and he died in hospital and all that's left is his little body. It can't hear or see, and it can't run and play. But that part of Timothy that knew you and loved you is not dead.' I was struggling and it was plain for all to see.

'He's gone to be with Jesus,' said a strident voice from a small boy whose hair looked as if he had just removed his fingers from an electric socket. It completely broke the tension.

'Yes,' I smiled at him, 'that's exactly where he is, but there is something more.' They looked at me as my voice became animated, as it does whenever I'm with children. 'One day Jesus will stand beside this very same box, long after we have put it in the ground. He will put His hand on the lid, just like this,' I replaced my hand, 'and say, "Little boy, I say to you, get up." He has done it before, you know.' I was thinking of Jairus' daughter. 'And do you know what?' I looked at the children; they were engrossed. 'He will. Timothy will come out of this box. He will have a new body, just like Jesus came out of His tomb when He rose from the dead on the first Easter Sunday. Look here,' I said, 'the Bible tells us that when Jesus comes back, we who love him will become like new. And those who have died before us will also become like new. New bodies. I know it's very hard to understand, but not all living things are the same. They don't have the same body, and when Timmy comes back he will have a new body.' I was beginning to lose them again. 'Touch each other,' I said. 'Go on, touch each other's arms and heads and noses.' They began to join in. 'It's all skin, isn't it? Now look at this.' I moved to a box-like object on a table and removed the covering cloth. In its cage a bright yellow canary hopped from one perch to another. 'He's got feathers,' I said with a triumphant voice. 'That's different to you. Look at this one, it's got scales, yuk!'

pulling off a second cover to reveal my goldfish, 'and this one has got hair and a flat face.' To the gasps of delight from the children, my son Richard entered. Cradled in his arms was Adam, our ten-week-old English bulldog puppy, all fur and skin and wrinkles. Richard sat down among the children as they began to stroke and prod the little dog. 'Now, do you see, when Timothy comes back he too will have a different body.' Reaching for my Bible, I read to the assembled children and adults the short passage from 1 Corinthians 15.

'Oh yes, we have a hope,' I said, pausing to look away from a young woman whose face shone through the streaming tears. To have continued looking at her would have broken me completely. 'And that hope is there in spite of the pain of loss. And in spite of what seems so hopeless, I know that nothing can separate us from the love of God that is in Christ Jesus. And I know that he will raise us up on the last day.'

The service was noisy and bitter-sweet, but it was exactly what Timothy's parents had wanted. 'We can't thank you enough,' they said later, as together with Richard and Adam the five of us made a poignant picture outside the church. Just over a year later we would remember that day as they clung on to me at Richard's funeral, reliving their grief as they shared in mine.

9

A Ministry Collapses

O LORD my God, I take refuge in you;
  save and deliver me from all who pursue me,
  or they will tear me like a lion.

(Ps. 7:1–2)

Richard sought a rough form of justice of his own when he was about sixteen. He had been out with some friends who had been taunting him about his new hairstyle, if that's the way you want to describe it. It had been cropped really short at school by a classmate who had dared Richard to allow him to use an electric shaver and produce a skinhead effect. You need to understand that Richard had this thing about his hair. It was very fair and usually of more than reasonable length. He was something of a turn on to the girls and took some pride in the way his hair looked, often looking in the mirror and flicking it back through his fingers. Now suddenly it was gone, removed in a stroke by some unkind machine. When I first saw him after the event I did not recognise who he was. It was shocking to see my son almost bald. What struck me most was the way the lack of hair accentuated his ears as well as his nose, making them look much larger than life. I remember babbling how different he looked, and being all the more surprised when he seemed to be pleased about the effect. I couldn't imagine why he felt this way; as far as I was concerned he had somewhat lost his good looks.

'What do you think, Dad? Cool, hey?'

'No, Rick, I don't think it's cool. I think it's a mess. How could you be so stupid? What possessed you?'

All this did not worry him at all because he had won new favour with his peers. He had risen to a dare as only a few in his class could do and was now something of a hero – a strange form of heroism, but that's sixteen-year-olds for you. However, after a week or so one of his friends began to taunt him playfully about his ears, saying that he looked like a Volkswagen Beetle with the doors left open. This, in the presence of a few pretty maidens, was enough for Richard to dish out his own form of punishment; yelling, he chased the friend for five or six blocks before dive-tackling him on to a grass verge and pinning him to the ground. Then, securing him in a headlock, Richard marched him into a nearby garden and banged on the door of the house. A startled elderly lady appeared.

'May I please use your hose?' asked my son. The lady looked at these two strange boys, one pleading, the other threatening, and was most alarmed.

'I'll call the police, I'll call the police!' she shouted round the chained half-open door.

'Thanks anyway,' said Richard and proceeded to turn the hose on his struggling friend to the cheers of the small crowd that had followed the chase and now stood at the garden gate. It was a moment of triumph for both of them as they fell into a saturated heap on the grass. 'Revenge,' he yelled at the sky, 'is so-o-o sweet.'

This story was related to me a week or so after Richard's

funeral, as tears streamed down the face of the now seventeen-year-old boy who had wrestled a garden hose together with the friend he had just lost to terrorist gunmen.

The incident with the garden hose came at a time when I was having my own difficulties in the new ministry we had returned to in Cape Town nearly two years earlier.

Almost from the start I did not get along with some of the members of my church council. Looking back, I now realise that I was the wrong man in the wrong place at the wrong time. On top of that I received little support from ministerial colleagues in dealing with the problems. Many were having similar problems themselves.

When a minister gets to a point in his ministry where he realises that certain forces are actively trying to remove him from his office, life becomes rather like standing over a trap door, waiting for the bolt to be pulled back opening a gap into a bottomless pit. I felt just like that after a protracted tension had arisen between me and my church elders, something which happens now and then in many a ministry.

I had taken advice from some older churchmen as how best to conduct myself and lead my church.

'When I arrived at my new church I told them that there was a new boss in town,' said one of them recklessly.

'You must not let them push you around,' said another. 'When I wanted to hold a service in a local community hall I got a lot of flak from some people. I simply told them that if they wanted to meet at the church that Sunday it would be fine with me, but *I* would be preaching down the road.' (Notice the first person singular in both cases – it sums up the situation rather well.) This advice demonstrated a strange kind of bravado and may have not been entirely honest, but foolishly, and to a lesser extent, I took it. Of course, it backfired.

In many churches you will find those who get involved for the power and prestige it brings. Others regard it as something of a club and as 'doing one's bit for the community'. Some tend to forget that it is primarily a position of servitude, something you can easily see at certain council meetings. I don't believe it would serve the cause of Christ to catalogue my grievance, for I am sure that there would be those who would be only too willing to remind me of my own failings, of which, I must be the first to admit, there were many. But one thing must be said. I believe that difficulties arose when I began to call the leaders of the church – the deacons or, if you prefer, the PCC – to be seen to be leading, to attend church services regularly and to be seen at Bible studies and prayer meetings. Although I might not have expected all this from ordinary members of the congregation, I did feel these activities should be part of a church leader's responsibility.

Matters had come to a head and I sought advice from a minister friend who had problems with his own eldership. We met one morning for coffee.

'Miles,' I said, as we sat together in a little coffee shop in Claremont, 'I'm preaching my heart out every Sunday. I put every ounce of effort into it. By Monday morning I'm exhausted.'

'I know the feeling.' Miles sighed and stared out of the window at the passing traffic.

'I'm trying to be true to my calling. I believe I'm faithful to the Bible – at least no one has accused me of being unbiblical, not to my face at any rate. I spend hours each week in preparation. I even go to bed at eight thirty every Saturday night so as to be better prepared for Sunday.'

'Ooh! Perhaps I should get you a larger cap for when you go to rugby next time.' He grinned and I felt suitably chastised. I stared at the steam rising from my mug.

'I don't mean that, I mean –'

'I know exactly what you mean,' he interrupted, 'and I also know that none of us do this to get any thanks. But we ought to get a bit more support from our own ranks. It's a hard enough battle fighting those from without, let alone having to take on insiders at the same time.' He paused and scratched his beard. 'Have any of them started having secret meetings yet?'

'I think so,' I said, 'a few of them.'

'Well, I came across one of my guys going through my private desk last week. Said he was looking for baptism records. But I know that there are some who want me to move to another part of the country.' I shook my head. I would like to add 'in disbelief', but I knew all too well now that these things happened. Miles continued, 'I was told yesterday that if I didn't do what I was told, I would be "crushed". That was the exact word.'

'What!' This time it was disbelief. 'You're kidding! That's not the way Christian leaders talk.'

'It's not the way normal people talk. I think some of these people watch too much television. Anyway, you can check it out with Kate; she heard it, too.' Miles looked at me, and then stared at a picture on the wall. 'You remember what happened to Rodney.'

'Only too well,' I replied, as my mind went back to a time in my first few years as an ordained clergyman, when Miles and I witnessed an elderly and godly man being hounded out of ministry because just one person believed that he should not be there. 'No one came to his aid,' I said ruefully.

'And no one will come to yours,' said Miles.

'I know,' I replied.

'Not even the ones you trust the most,' said Miles prophetically.

'I know that, too. A letter signed by everyone on the council has been sent to the bishops, and a copy shoved under my door. Not even the grace to give it to me in person.'

'What does it say?'

I took it out of my pocket and pushed it across the table. 'A classic case of the sheep leading the shepherd,' said Miles after a while. 'But this bit,' he paused and refilled his mug, 'about spending less time in your pulpit and how you should be spending your week. Why, they have even broken down each day into time-bites. Do they think you are an imbecile or something?'

'Must do. Look at the signatures.'

'What are you going to do?'

'I don't know yet.' I think there were tears in his eyes. 'I just don't know.'

Two weeks later I resigned But had I done the right thing? I was seized with doubt.

A short while after my resignation a council member phoned and asked if he could come and talk to me. As matters were tense I was reluctant to discuss anything without an impartial mediator present. This the caller knew, but he assured me that he 'just wanted to see how I was doing'. In this he sounded gracious. He duly arrived, now accompanied by a second council member, and the meeting went ahead despite my discomfort. With hindsight perhaps I should have refused to see them, but that would have been churlish. I felt some tension but on the whole I believe the meeting was conducted amicably by all sides. That was not the problem.

It was about an hour after we had parted that I went into my secretary's office. She was out for a moment and I turned over one or two sheets of paper on her desk in search of something I had given her. There before me lay a handwritten transcript, minutes if you like, of the meeting the three of us had had earlier. It was formal, stating date, place, time and persons present. I could not believe what I was reading. No notes had been taken during the meeting and there was certainly no notice given that any would be. After all, it had been a meeting to 'see how I was doing'. Attached was a note to my secretary instructing her to type the minutes and return them to the gentlemen concerned. They were not to be given to me.

Much of what was discussed was indeed recorded, but not all, and there were many inaccuracies. At the very least, the meeting I had attended was not fully reflected in the notes. I had a strong impulse to rip the pages up. Perhaps I should have done it, or maybe confronted the men concerned about their devious behaviour. I did neither. I simply replaced the pieces of paper on the desk and walked back into my office. I picked up the phone to Miles. I was now certain that I had done the right thing.

As Miles had foretold, no one came to my aid. I could not with a clear conscience be told when to preach, how to preach, how long to spend in preparation, how and when I should counsel and to make private counselling records available for others to scrutinise. Those with the power lust and the will to control had, to my mind, stepped over the line. Judas had planted his kiss and I felt angry, bitter and betrayed. The years of my training stood for nothing as other church leaders avoided the conflict. Too busy with their own problems, they no doubt decided it was more expedient to pass by on the other side. Now I had to take the bitter pill of my own counsel, given time after time to others as they sat across my desk: the broken-hearted divorcee, the bereaved parent, the hurting ex-employee, and so on and on and on.

Most in the congregation didn't know of the conflict that was taking place behind the scenes and felt hurt and betrayed when I resigned. I stated my reasons to the church eldership but not to the congregation. It was inevitable that rumours would find very fertile soil in which to grow. One that was particularly painful was that Mary and I were having difficulties in our marriage and therefore had to leave the ministry – but nothing could have been further from the truth. Another was a letter pinned to the church notice board stating that we needed a break from ministry and would return after a two-year leave of absence. That was an outright lie, as I had never discussed any leave of absence, of whatever duration, with anyone. Quite simply, the letter had been put up to keep people quiet.

Our children found it difficult not to be involved. They too were affected greatly as they found that they could no longer take part in youth activities. Here, Richard, with typically flamboyant teenage ebullience, offered his counsel.

'Stuff them, Dad! Who needs them, anyway?' I was horrified at my son's outburst. But the truth was we did need them. The trouble for me was that they didn't need us. Neither, it seemed, did they want us. That was the hardest thing for my own stupid pride to swallow. Not one person in the entire congregation raised his or her voice loud enough to say, 'What's going on here?' Not one.

Emotion raged within. I was both betrayer and betrayed. The anger I felt for the few men who had begun the work of ousting me was huge. They had cost me my home and my ministry. I had done an unpardonable thing in that I had called the spiritual leaders to account in stressing the need for them to demonstrate their spirituality and be seen to be involving themselves in the life of the church. It was a bridge too far.

I very soon discovered at first hand that unemployment hits ministers in the same way as it hits everyone else. For the first week or so, I felt overcome by what might be called a low-grade depression and a sense of helplessness. I would yell at the kids for no reason, and the one who saw the brunt of my anger most was Richard. There were times when I seemed paralysed by inactivity. I would jump when the phone rang, but rarely answered it. The assurances of friends seemed so hollow. 'It's easy for you to talk of the faithfulness of God. You still have a job,' I would think to myself.

Such was the nature of the beast I was facing that I had neither the heart nor the stomach for a conflict of this magnitude, and so I quit. In so doing I felt as if I had betrayed my calling, my congregation, my family and my God. Feelings of guilt and failure washed over me as I trudged the streets looking for some form of employment. A sinkhole of self-pity engulfed me as I sold household insurance while we prepared to return to England. In six months' time my home would be in a cardboard box in storage, and my son would be dead.

It is impossible to give advice to others on how to deal with crises. Each set of circumstances is so different. How I dealt with it may not be appropriate to anyone else. I remember preaching from Hebrews 11 some years earlier on faith and trusting God. Now I was expected to put into practice all that I had preached. It was a real case of 'physician, heal thyself'. I was the pastor who now needed a pastor, and few were to be found. Certainly there were none among my former colleagues.

'Let it go,' was the advice I had given Roger Page, some time earlier. 'If you don't, the anger and bitterness will turn in on you and destroy you.' I hated myself for those words. Of course they were true, but I didn't want to follow them to the letter. I wanted to hurt someone for all the pain and betrayal I had endured and, to my great shame, I wanted harm to come to them for what they had done and allowed to be done to me and my family. But there was, in fact, nothing I could do. God would be watching me, even if no one else was. For my own part, I could do nothing but let it go and leave it to God.

Yes, my passions were high, but I made a deliberate choice not to take any action that I felt I might regret later. I was forced to turn to God and pour all my anger and frustration on Him. He promised that revenge was His for the taking, and I was going to take Him at His word. In my subsequent dealings with others who have been aggrieved or hurt, forgiveness is one of the hardest things to come to terms with. One mother, whose little daughter was raped and murdered, still seeks vengeance even though the person responsible was caught and sentenced to life in prison. It is etched into her face. Twenty-five years on, she still cannot sleep at night and any talk of clemency sends her into fits of rage, tears and unbelievable stress. She has said that to let it go would be unfaithful to her little girl's memory. I too have lost a child: I can say – in fact, have a right to say – that the child is gone from this life, and if we are to be faithful to the memory of one so dear, so precious, then we owe it to them, if not to ourselves, to live life as fully as we are able. We cannot do that if we nurture a spirit of revenge, and they, who loved us much in this life, would not wish to see our lives so incapacitated. There are also others around us who will be watching the way we conduct ourselves, and our influence on them is just as important. Life must go on in spite of the hurts and blows. While we will never forget those we have lost, time does dull the pain. But only if we let it.

10

Pastors Under Pressure

Time, time, time – see what's become of me.
(Paul Simon)

Pastors are no longer burnt at the stake as they were in
Reformation times, but many are certainly being burnt
out. Today, more than at any time, pastoral ministry
is characterised by stress and strain. I believe there are
a number of factors which pastors need to reflect upon
before 'giving up' on ministry. With hindsight, I think
that I might have caved in too easily. Had these issues
been more clearly defined while I was in training at college
and later as a curate, or had I had stronger support groups,
things might have been very different. One must remember
that the tangible support of the clergy is a vital factor. The
pulpit must be protected.

I knew about the visibility of the minister's role when I
entered the ministry, but what I had not realised was the
closeness with which he and his family are observed. The
minister is continually on display. The behaviour of his
children, the profile of his wife and even the clothes he
wears are constantly under scrutiny. If he buys a new
sports jacket, he is being flamboyant. If he wears his old

one, he is too shabby. If his wife has a new hairdo, he is being paid too much. If she neglects it, she looks like a picture in a Victorian missionary magazine.

There are countless stories of how so-called PKs (preachers' kids) have rebelled and become wild and disobedient. Both of our daughters feel a sense of relief that Mary and I are no longer in full-time ministry. Recently a minister told of the occasion when he took a part-time job to fund his children's university education, only to be told by his bishop that he had to realise that there were some sacrifices that he had to make in his calling and that the ongoing education of his children was one of them. Needless to say, the bishop could afford to educate his children in a manner appropriate to their future, and the minister concerned is now no longer in full-time ministry.

Unlike most other professions, there is a very close connection between the pastor's work and his personal life. Even kings, princes and presidents can have extra-marital affairs and still keep their jobs. But woe betide the minister should his marriage or family life not be ideal. It has become 'unwise' to counsel females, especially young, single and attractive, on their own. The door of his study should remain open and a third party should be close by. Should he be driving along the road in his car and a female parishioner need a lift, it becomes expedient for him 'not to see her' or to deliberately pass by. And the reason? Not so much the weakness of the flesh but the wagging of the tongue.

There is a high expectancy placed upon pastors which has become, to use the current phrase, 'market driven'. Society's yardstick measures you by your achievements. This measure is now being used of the Church.

The pastor needs to remind himself that he is still part of

the human race. He is not some super-spiritual hero who
is never to show his weakness. Wearing an elite mask not
only puts undue stress on him and his family, but also
gives an unrealistic image to those he ministers to. If he is
prepared to acknowledge his humanity, then the goings-on
in his household will have less interest for those around
him. He will truly be seen as 'one of us'. Sadly, there are
some ministers to whom this notion is an anathema.

In human terms, it is the minister who is seen as the 'head'.
When things go wrong in the church the buck has to stop
with him. There is no one else. If the church is empty, it is his
fault. If disgruntled parishioners move, he is responsible. If
the funds are down, he has 'got to do something', anything,
except hold a raffle or a barn dance. If his sermons have
any jokes, he is flippant. If not, he is dull. If he preaches
on sin, he is a prophet of doom. If he preaches on social
and political issues, then he is 'not sticking to the Truth'.
The often quoted jibe – What did you have for lunch on
Sunday? Answer, roast chicken and roast minister – is not
too far from the truth. He becomes a scapegoat for those
who are quick to criticise but slow to act.

Alas for some, ministers who fail to meet the expectations
of their church may be asked or forced to leave. Some
churches can be fairly brutal if their pastors are not
'successful'.

Yet if members of the congregation truly play their part
in serving God and the Church, there is no need for the
minister to be treated as a scapegoat, but rather as a
member of the team. Most problems and pressures arise
when the pastor takes everything upon himself.

*   *   *

But how then is this success measured in a society that demands some tangible proof? If a salesman does not sell his product, he is dismissed. If a company director is not producing growth, he is hauled up in front of the shareholders. If a politician is incompetent, he is not re-elected (some, at any rate). But what of the minister? What is it that measures his success? A full church? A bulging treasury? Hordes of weeping, penitent sinners flocking to his pulpit begging God for mercy? Some would think so.

But let him spend a morning grappling in prayer for his people with the door of his study closed, and he may easily find himself accused of not spending time with old Mrs Jones who needs him at one of her tea parties. Sunday sermons, after all, can be prepared on Saturday – after the late-night movie.

Some have said that the only areas in which a minister can see a tangible result for his efforts are those of fund-raising or building projects. At the end of the day, with market forces, such as they are, gathered around him, it may be that this is the only way he can stand back and survey his efforts with satisfaction. But edifices of this nature are often nothing more than monuments to one man's ego. There are places around the world where churches are spending thousands if not millions on buildings, while within a twenty-mile radius of their structures people are dying of illness or starvation.

The pastor needs to remember that the Lord did not call him to be successful, but to be faithful. It is faithfulness that will result in fruitfulness. It is required of stewards to be trustworthy.

Unlike most who trudge off to earn their daily bread, the minister does not have any set hours. He cannot put down his pen or turn off his computer at the end of a nine-to-five day and go home. He 'lives above the shop', and because of the nature of his work there is never a moment when he is truly 'off'.

There are always demands on his time as there is always something to be done. If the minister is not careful, he can easily acquire a guilty conscience as expectations of ministry become unrealistic. There is the well-known story of the questionnaire given to the members of one particular church in which they were asked how their minister should spend his day. They were also asked to estimate how long he should spend per week on matters such as sermon preparation, counselling, administration, youth work, etc. When the figures were collected and added up, it was discovered that 82 hours was the average working time expected. One reply even suggested 200 hours, though the total number of hours in a week is only 168!

Families can only add to the pressure. Countless children have said to their ministering fathers, 'You always have time for others . . . you never have time for me.'

When Moses led the Israelites through the desert for forty years he became exhausted by the fact that he was taking on too much responsibility. Wisely his father-in-law counselled him to share the work with others. It is estimated that many thousands were involved in leadership of one form or another.

The often misquoted phrase, 'money is the root of all evil', illustrates one of the reasons that pastors are paid so poorly. The problem is not 'the money' but the *love* of it. Money is amoral. It has no intrinsic morality. Money is, in a sense, life. We all need it if we are to survive in our society but, like anything else, the desire of it can lead to abuse.

The apostle Paul told the young Timothy to take a glass of wine for his stomach ailment. There is absolutely nothing wrong with a glass of wine. However, the abuse of wine has been exceedingly destructive, as with many things that God intended for our enjoyment. Money, because of its power, is one of them. 'Keep him humble and pay him less' is the syndrome that clergy have suffered over the years. I don't believe anyone can do his job properly if his mind is on his overdue electricity bill. And when you get the super-spiritual who intone: 'Aahh, the man must have faith, brother,' I respond and say, 'Rubbish!' An effective pastor will be supported by the generous and responsible giving of God's people. If money just grew out of the ground, no one would have a problem. Congregations have forgotten that their income ultimately comes from God. Even those on the dole!

Compounding the problem is the matter of housing. Many clergy today have to make their own arrangements when they come to retire, and as most have been living in church houses all their working lives, to be vacated upon retirement or resignation, many have had to endure additional stress. In some areas, the Church is oblivious to this. And in many cases marriages and relationships suffer.

John Stanford, an Anglican psychologist, in his work *Ministry Burnout* describes the task as never-ending. Quite naturally this can only add to the pressure. He writes:

The carpenter, for instance, finishes the table he is making; the engineer can stand back and admire the bridge he has built; the surgeon may have the satisfaction of seeing his patient recover; the lawyer will eventually wind up the case with which he has been wrestling. Not so the ministering person. The ministering person is like Sisyphus in Greek mythology, whose fate it was to have to push a great stone up a mountain only to have it roll down again before reaching the top. This feeling that the job is endless, that you can never quite reach the top of the mountain, no matter how hard you try, can lead to exhaustion.

In addition to all this, the minister has to fend off the growing theological quagmire that is a never-ending fashion. There have always been challenges to theology; even in the garden of Eden the serpent challenged Adam's theology. But it seems that today, more than ever, there is a growth of 'experts'. They seem to think that as they have now 'read a new book' they are an authority on the Bible. The notion that you have to *study* is being replaced in certain circles with a superior spirituality that says, 'God told me'.

If I were to read a book on quantum physics and then tell a university professor that there was little he could teach me because I had 'read a book', he would dismiss me as a fool, and rightly so. But today ministers have to treat with tolerance many such fools. And they must do it with grace, lest they be charged with being unloving. The same charge is made against clergy who refuse to marry people who have no interest in attending church other than for the marriage ceremony. It is also made against ministers who will not officiate at baptisms where the participants only want to go through the ritual of it all and have no interest in spiritual things.

Without doubt, the greatest pressure that the pastor must endure is his continual battle against the forces of darkness – the spiritual battle, the inner battle, where his character before God is forged on the fire and sweat of prayer. He is in the front line of this battle. It is here that his walk with God must be most closely attended. It is his greatest need; it is his Achilles' heel. He may be disclosing the truth to his congregation, week in and week out, but unless he spends time alone with his Boss he will stumble along as if he had a stone in his shoe. This one area alone, the area that can be cut back on most readily, is the very area that must not be neglected. The builder can be kept waiting for a moment, the treasurer can shuffle paper in the outer office, the irate parishioner can continue to pace the carpet in the corridor if he or she chooses, even dear old Mrs Jones can have another tea party another time, but God must not be kept at arm's length. *He must not.* The pastor must make an appointment with his Lord every day and stick to it as if his life depended on it – as it does. I say to my shame that I cancelled many of these appointments. And I did so to my cost.

There are, of course, many other pressures that the minister must endure and the above list is by no means exhaustive. The growing threat from cults; the shortage of skills, manpower and funds; the onslaught of modern technology as the young are swamped by watching, rather than listening and reading; the falling and fickle morality of a society that is all too quick to tell us that the Bible is outdated and obsolete: all these will take their toll. But the one area lacking most in so many churches is that of pastoral support. Who pastors the pastors? Who sits beside the weeping priest, the devastated missionary and the broken bishop? Chapter 11 will tell of my own experience, and I know of many who have been abandoned by the Church, who have been 'relegated to the second division' because they do not have the same public profile, whose PCCs, elderships, diaconates, wardens and overseers are too busy or just not bothered. These men and women have crept on to church councils because of their personal wealth or status in society and 'want to do their bit'. They stand as pillars of their society, but simply turn and run or melt like chocolate soldiers when the going becomes too hot. My father-in-law once said of these people, 'It makes me want to spit.' I agree with him.

One area that Jesus attacked vociferously was that of hypocrisy. He told the religious leaders of his day that they were nothing but white-washed sepulchres, nice on the outside but dead, dead, dead. There are many leaders in the Church who fall into this category, across all denominations. They are arrogant, self-assured and self-righteous. Even if St Paul were to rise from the dead and write a letter to them today, they would probably throw it into the bin.

After all this, the question that must present itself is this: Is it worth the time, effort and strain to join the ministry? The answer is simple. It is the highest call that a human being can aspire to. To serve God full time, to pour all your energy into His kingdom and His people and to take it on the chin when attacked, is the greatest work a man or woman can do. Its endeavours are eternal. Its effects are everlasting. 'How beautiful are the feet of him who brings good news.' And the gospel of Christ *is* good news. Even if the world does not know it. Even if the Church at large does not recognise it. But the stakes are high. It cost the Son of God His life to bring us closer to the Father, and all too often ministers fall, broken and bruised, along the way, with none but God to pick them up as they try to bring people closer to the Son.

11

Storm Ride

How long, O Lord? Will you forget me for ever?
How long will you hide your face from me?
                                                    (Ps. 13:1)

Richard's Christianity often came into conflict with his teen
years. At times the two seemed incompatible. At times he
was the frustrated, angry young man who just wanted his
freedom and saw us, his parents, as a bulwark against his
plans and desires to further that freedom. But then there
were other times when he was amazingly gentle and caring.
He loved and cared for his English bulldogs. He had great
respect for friendship and especially for loyalty within that
friendship. I remember how hurt he was when a friend of
his turned away from him because he didn't have the 'right
sort' of bike. He felt betrayed. And how he wept over the
telephone because he and a girlfriend had broken up.

He and I had our disagreements and more than our share
of arguments. Now, looking back, they seem so trivial, but
at the time they caused some tension. He often seemed to
get into trouble with his sisters and we would come down
hard on him. He used to enjoy watching the most appalling
movies of violence and horror, sitting on the edge of a chair
with his toes curled under his feet and his fingers jammed

into his ears. I used to remonstrate with him that it was not the sort of thing Christians should do, as what you fill your mind with can often emerge in your lifestyle.

'But why, Dad? I enjoy them,' would be his reply. I was dismayed but in some strange way I admired his honesty. I wanted to watch them myself, only, for a pastor, it wasn't the done thing. Had I watched them, I could not with integrity or impunity harangue an audience from the pulpit for watching 'non-Christian rubbish'. I remember once chiding a congregation on a particular topic only to be told by my son that 'you do that yourself'. Children can be more brutal than any morning mirror. They see you warts and all. How much more so does God in heaven.

On 6th December 1992, I handed over the keys to my office and car. I had no serious job prospects as the country was in the grip of recession and few churches would be interested in a man who, as it was told, had deserted his post. On top of that rumours abounded about the state of my marriage. However, we were allowed to stay on in the rectory for as long as it took the church to find another minister; this also suited the church treasurer, as he received rent. On 19th December, Mary's father died in Devon, after a long and difficult illness. We received the news on the day we were preparing to give our elder daughter, Amanda, an early twenty-first birthday party.

Amanda had just graduated from university. On 2nd January, she left to take up a job in Paris, and in the few weeks that followed her departure we came to the conclusion that it might be more appropriate for us to return to England and start afresh. Devon would provide a base where we could enrol Richard and Catherine in school and explore the prospect of jump-starting our ministry again after it had stalled. At the same time, we would be able to care for Mary's mother after her loss.

Late in June 1993, I had the opportunity to go on ahead to London to explore some prospects. Mary and Catherine would arrive in July, Amanda was already living in Paris and Richard would follow in November, meanwhile remaining in Cape Town to finish his Matric exams. On Sunday 25th July, two weeks after Mary and Catherine had left, at about 7.28 p.m., terrorists entered the church he had gone to with his host Pat Haram and murdered eleven people, wounding scores of others. Richard died shielding two girlfriends from the grenade blasts and machine-gun fire.

Back in Cape Town once again, on 27th July, sitting in the garden of the house we were loaned, we surveyed the wreckage and wondered if there was a God who cared.

Well, there was. He cared then and He still does, it's just that sometimes we are too blinded by our own pain to see it. Many friends gathered around us as tangible proof of God's care. There were generous financial gifts which helped put bread on the table, and we were even given the use of a car for as long as we needed.

A friend who is also a successful businessman sat with me over lunch one day with his head in his hands.

'I looked in on my own sons last night, Clive, and I don't know how I would cope if it were me in your shoes.' Tears filled his eyes.

'Just love them with all your might while you still can, Pete,' I replied. The pain in my throat was intense. 'We are all but a heartbeat away from God.' As we got to the car, he pushed an envelope into my hands.

'Open it later, please.'

I did. It contained a note and a cheque which helped us through the few months that followed. Yes, God does care. And so do His people.

What I dreaded was not that people would say silly things. We all do that when faced with tragedy, but if it is the heart that speaks then what is heard is more than the words. It is the isolation that is so hard to bear, that aloneness that is brought about by those who feel they have nothing to say and so stay away. Some of the most precious times were when people would say, 'I have nothing to say that will in any way ease your pain, I just want to share it with you.'

The very worst thing that anyone can ever say is, 'Don't worry, you'll get over it.' Death is awful and you never get over it. It is demonic and it stays with you until, I suppose, you face your own death. I have never got over Richard's death. I have got on, but not over. And if anyone reading this wants to take on the role of comforter and say such a stupid thing as, 'You'll get over it,' then they have removed themselves as far as is possible from the pain and are of no use at all. In order to be of comfort, one has to come close, so close you can touch the hurt yourself. I found very few who could do that.

However, at this point a special tribute needs to be made to the people and congregation of my former parish in Hillcrest, Natal. They were so concerned for us that they flew Mary and me to Durban for a short time of recovery. They provided a home for us, and met all our needs. We spent time with each other and with God as we walked the foothills of the magnificent Drakensberg mountain range. How many times we asked ourselves the question, 'why us?' I do not know. There was never any tangible reply, of course, but amid the physical and emotional pain we found comfort in each other.

Two other people were of great help. One was a Christian psychologist, Dr Christo C., who had taken a weekend retreat while I was rector of the church in Hillcrest in 1988, and the other was Mark Atherstone, who was my rector's warden during the first year of our stay in Natal. In 1989 Mark and his wife, Morag, had moved to the Natal midlands to manage a huge cattle farm.

Dr Christo taught me two things in the short time we were together. Christians had actively tried to destroy his own ministry in the Dutch Reformed Church, and he had learned that when our expectations of others are too high we are bound to be disappointed. Perhaps I had expected too much from some, and when, in my opinion, they were found wanting, my reaction was predictable. I have now taken this lesson into my own life and find it invaluable. It is true that many pastors can expect too much from their congregations and become angry and frustrated when these expectations are not met. Often sermons then become points of grind against those who haven't come up to scratch. All too often, it is the willing few who get lumbered with most of the work and then become exhausted. Clergy too easily forget that lay people have responsibilities outside the church and can lay a burden of guilt on some which is unwise, unnecessary and unbiblical.

The second thing Dr Christo showed us was what to expect from God in times of difficulty. Expect Him to care. His Word promises it: He says, 'I will never leave you nor forsake you.' This is easier said than done, but it does become a matter of trust. In our hearts and minds we had to come to terms with forgiving those who had killed Richard as well as those who had seen to the demise of our ministry. While the words may have seemed hollow and empty, even hypocritical, in prayer we offered to God our thanks for the memories of our son and our forgiveness for his killers. Does that mean I feel that they should get off scot-free? No, it doesn't. I believe that in a civilised society the law must be upheld, and must be seen to be upheld. As part of the concept of a godly society, those who do evil must be punished by the state and so be a warning for those who wish to do evil – a deterrent, if you like. In this regard I am in complete agreement with the family of Steve Biko, the black activist who was murdered in police custody in South Africa. His killers have appealed to the Truth and Reconciliation Committee for amnesty. I believe they should be brought to justice, just as I feel Richard's killers should. My forgiveness for them is my choice, but their crime must still be accounted for. This is beyond my power to achieve.

We left Dr Christo no lighter in spirit, but, I believe, more honest. We had offered God our forgiveness of others, and had meant it. The pain we carried would diminish in time, but not if we continued to bear a spirit of vengeance.

It was a little later that same week that I sat with Mark Atherstone in the garden of his farmhouse.

'I've got so little to say to you, Clive,' he said, as we looked out on to the magnificent view together. 'It's as if I am watching the aftermath of a train wreck. I just don't know what to say.' Many felt the same way as Mark. Good heavens, I had felt just like that myself many times

113

in pastoral ministry. But I have learnt that just being there is often enough.

'It's strange, but in my prayer-time yesterday . . .' Oh no, I thought, more of God speaking to someone else, but not me. It was wrong of me because Mark is not that sort of man and doesn't express his feelings that easily. He continued, 'It was about Jesus sending His disciples across the lake. He knew what was going to happen to them, the storm I mean, but He sent them nonetheless.' Mark paused as one of his sons came charging up to show his daddy a toy that needed repair. My mind raced back to another place, another time and another little boy with shining eyes. I swallowed the lump in my throat with coffee from the table. 'Yes, David, but go and put it on the work bench. We will fix it later.' The lad scampered off. 'Why did he do that?' I looked at him, bemused. He continued, 'Jesus, I mean? He told them to go and they went, but what was to follow was a time of terror.'

'I suppose they still had lessons to learn. Like trust.' I thought for a moment. 'We choose our Lord but we don't always choose our path.'

'Yes,' Mark said thoughtfully. 'Only they didn't know that at the time.'

'We're not talking about a storm that will last a few hours, Mark. It seems to have no end to it. And as tragic as it was, Richard's death wasn't the start. It began at least a year before that.' I got up and walked across to an old tree stump and picked at the rotting bark.

'That's the point, Clive. Time is not the issue. An hour, a day, a month or some years. You have something to learn in the midst of this storm, and neither of us knows what that is right now.' He came over to me, carrying my coffee. 'Neither, I suppose, did those fishermen, at the time.'

'And some of them weren't even fishermen. Must have been tougher on them,' I mused.

Thank God for men like Mark Atherstone in Natal and Ashley Smyth in Cape Town: mooring posts in the teeth of the hurricane.

Ashley was the pastor of an independent fellowship. He would be at our home at two in the morning when we needed him, picking up the pieces and trying to stick them together. But for some reason, the people with whom I once worked and served in ministry never contacted me or my wife. I know that they weren't, but it certainly seemed as if they were uninterested. We had lost a ministry, a home and a son, all in the space of six months. Some would see me in the street and cross over to the other side or suddenly take an interest in a shop window containing piping and guttering. Certainly, there were old friends who did call and express support and concern, but the surprising thing was that, for the most part, church leadership beheld the spectacle and then seemed to 'pass by on the other side'.

Less than four months after I had laid my son's ashes to rest, I was accused by this same leadership of letting the church down. I will never know what was said behind my back, but to my face I was called an enigma, a maverick and one who could not be of any service because I did not realise the depth of my own grief. I don't suppose that I will ever know what it is that causes some Christians to say such things to another, especially to one already weakened spiritually and emotionally. Instead of having an arm around my shoulder, it felt as if I had a fist in my stomach. It was crass and cruel.

As the song says, 'Brother, let me be your servant' – hmmm!

Incredible as it may sound, it is entirely possible that the feelings I had for the perpetrators of my son's death were overshadowed by the distress caused to me and my family by the apparent lack of concern of some members of the Christian community. The former were faceless, nameless and cruel, and knew no better. The latter were once friends, colleagues and those who had a system of values related to them Sunday by Sunday from lofty platforms. Too bad that both preacher and people alike would not put these principles into practice. I felt utterly betrayed and let down, and may well have displaced much of my anger towards the Church. It was even worse when someone from my former circle of associates began to verbally undermine both the fellowship that was now my new spiritual home and also its pastor for interfering. It seemed that whatever I did, I just could not win.

However, it is important to realise that the Church of God is an imperfect place, filled with and led by imperfect people. We all fall short, even those who strive to be utterly faithful to the integrity and preaching of the Word of God. But it is equally important to realise that God should not take the blame for this. It is the example of His Son we should emulate, not His servants. There have been many times that I have let people down, times I am too ashamed to recall.

I do not recount all these facts to keep people from church – quite the opposite. It is within these very walls and from these very pulpits that the love and mercy of God can be made known and made manifest. My family and I came to know of the love of God from within these same walls. It was I who failed God and my congregation, and if others were honest they would make the same claim.

It was the uneasy reaction of politicians in South Africa that finally caused me to leave the land of my birth and return to the land of my fathers. I had stated in one newspaper article that, if possible, I would have preferred to stay in South Africa and help, in however small a way. The political situation was very tense indeed in 1993.

It was a matter of weeks after the funeral, when the dust was beginning to settle, that I put pen to paper and wrote to the eight most prominent politicians in the country: the President of South Africa, F.W. de Klerk; Nelson Mandela of the ANC; Mangosuthu Buthelezi of Inkatha; Clarence Makwetu of the PAC; Eugene Terre'Blanche of the Afrikaner Resistance Movement; Constand Viljoen of the Afrikaner Volksfront; Zac de Beer of the Democratic Party, and Ferdie Hartzenberg of the Conservative Party. My name had been in every newspaper, my face on national television. My seventeen-year-old son had been murdered by political terrorists: I thought that in the light of the international media interest in the Cape Town Massacre I would receive a response from them, however small. I was wrong. My letter did not seek sympathy, but encouragement to remain in South Africa. Here is an extract:

> I write seeking your input at a time when our country is torn apart due to the random nature of hatred and violence . . . I do not seek your sympathy although I am sure you will offer it. My loss is all our loss but without your influence and help, I do not foresee a future for South Africa that will be free of bloodshed.

Only its leaders can influence the path that this country
will take and leaders must be seen to be leading, then
at grassroots people will feel secure and follow.

What would your proposal be to stop the violence
if it were only up to you? . . . I believe that I have
the right to ask.

My family and I had planned to settle in England
even though I am Cape Town born . . . I want to be
part of the solution, not add to this country's problem.
Please, how could you encourage me to stay?

I have no hatred or bitterness in me, only questions
and a sincere desire to see peace and civilised justice
prevail. My Christian ethic calls on me to seek peace
and the extension of God's Kingdom on earth.

Can you help me in my decision making?

Perhaps it is not surprising that five did not find the time
to reply and that of the three that did (Buthelezi, de Beer
and Viljoen) not one could encourage me to stay. It was yet
another blow to the many already received. Perhaps they
foresaw the escalation and growth of crime and violence
that, as I write some four years later, is now so widespread
in South Africa.

I have been accused by some of taking what is known
in South Africa as the 'Chicken Run'. A son murdered in
Cape Town, a cousin murdered in Johannesburg, a friend
murdered in Natal. Chicken run indeed, especially in a
country whose leaders could not or would not give any
sensible reason for me to stay. Hundreds of people are
still being killed each week – not each year, each week.
The cost of living is high; unemployment is over 30 per cent.
Phrases like 'affirmative action', 'no employer lockouts'

and 'state-owned banks', together with armed vigilantes roaming the streets, do little to encourage the greatly needed inflow of foreign investors. President Mandela's state visit to England and France in 1996 attracted much media attention, and justly so, for it was proper to honour this international statesman in his personal capacity. But businessmen need a lot more than seeing a president ride down the Mall in an open carriage with the Queen, or hearing a few impassioned speeches over an expensive luncheon, to encourage them to part with their cash.

But in December 1993 all this was a very long way from how I was feeling. And on a cold wet Christmas Day in a borrowed house back in London, Mary, Amanda, Catherine and I returned from church in Northwood and sat down to our first Christmas dinner without Richard. We might just as well have been eating dry cream crackers.

12

The Turning Point

Those who sow in tears
  will reap with songs of joy.
He who goes out weeping,
carrying seed to sow,
will return with songs of joy,
carrying sheaves with him.

(Ps. 126:5–6)

C.S. Lewis, in his book *A Grief Observed*, says, 'But go to
Him when your need is desperate, when all other help is
vain and what do you find? A door slammed in your face,
and a sound of bolting and double bolting on the inside.
After that, silence. You may as well turn away.'

A son dead. A country abandoned. A ministry lost. A home
all wrapped up in cardboard. My need was desperate, and
with little prospect of employment I became engulfed in
depression and self-pity. I would awake in the morning to
the sound of Mary enduring yet another of her frequent
panic attacks. They were horrendous and there was nothing
we could do but endure them. We certainly could not stop
them. What she must have suffered defies description.
  On one cold, wet, February North Devon morning, the

sun – whatever that was – had still not yet risen when, unable to bear Mary's anguish any longer, I slipped from bed and went into the sitting-room to rail against God – again. And again I got the usual wall of silence. Maybe I was too busy banging and crashing against heaven's door, making such a din of my own that I failed to hear the still, small voice of God. I just don't know. All I do know is that God seemed very far from me.

I had not been there very long when the door opened and there stood my wife. I was shocked. I could hardly recognise her. She looked as if she was dead. I have often seen dead people in my capacity as a pastor; I had seen my father after he had died, as well as my son. Now I stared into the vacant face of the woman I loved and with whom I had shared so much for so long. The light was quite literally gone from her eyes, and her face was a death mask. I was aghast. We sat on the sofa and held on to each other for dear life. There was nothing to look forward to; there seemed no hope in the future. Suicide did not occur to us then and never did thereafter, but looking back on those times I can understand why some take this route. Everything we knew was gone. All our foundations were shattered and shaken. We ached in our inner being. I was filled with hatred for my own actions that had brought us to this point, and for those who had propelled us along the way. It was as if I were watching my very life just pouring through my fingers, like so many grains of sand. How I longed for revenge. It would not, of course, have helped my situation one bit, but I wanted it nonetheless, even though I had offered God forgiveness some months before.

I had to endure these emotions and while I strongly felt

the need for some form of justice, some form of recompense, I knew, quite simply, that I had to let it go. But I didn't *want* to. I wanted to hurt someone, even if it were myself.

But however bleak things may be, however difficult the circumstances that surround one in times of despair, there comes a point when things do change. There is truth in the old adage that 'every cloud has a silver lining'. There *is* always light at the end of every tunnel, but as I also know full well, when you are in the middle of the tunnel nothing seems further from the truth.

The spirit of anger within me was strong, and the only way I could cope with it was to walk away. Believe me, this is not the coward's way out: it is the sane way, and I believe it is the right way, as human history is replete with tragedy because men and women wanted to get even. The feelings, of course, came with me as I walked; there was nothing I could do about them as they were generated from within the heart. It was quite useless to pretend that they did not exist – they did – but I believe that if I had harboured them, nurtured them or given them opportunity to take root, then they could have had their way with me and destroyed me.

When devastating pain hit me and my family, red-hot anger exploded like a lava-spewing volcano. Many may refuse to admit they have these intense feelings, or try to deny them altogether under the guise that Christians should not feel this way. It is not easy for a pastor to admit that hatred was a part of his life, but in my case, at times, it was. Passion is very much part of the human experience. A passion in hate is as natural as a passion in love. The question is how we control these passions.

I remember one woman saying to me with wide eyes and deliberate, measured tones, 'If my husband ever cheated on me, I would poison his tea and then tell God he got hit by a truck.' We can smile at this lady's threat, but since childhood we have all been told that anger, jealousy and hatred are bad emotions and that we should not have them. Well, God gets angry. God gets jealous and sad, and God does not have the 'advantage' of having a sinful nature to make excuses for such emotions. I know of some Christians who give the impression that all is well all the time. They say that they are never sick, angry, depressed or flustered. On one occasion I had the misfortune to tell a telephone enquirer that the object of his call was 'on the toilet' and asked if he could phone back later, only to be told quite strongly by the toilet sitter that I should have said that he was 'indisposed for a moment'. Some people just never like to give the impression of any weakness whatsoever and would probably call back from the coffin that they were temporarily inconvenienced.

The truth is that we all get angry, sad and sick. We all have to sit on that plastic (or wooden) round ring in the morning. We all suffer the weaknesses of the flesh, and to pretend otherwise is foolhardy. We can take pills for physical pain, but emotional hurts can go on and on and on and on. No pills help here. You can buy sleep from a bottle, but not rest. All we have in this regard is God, and we have to lean, and lean heavily, on Him. It was during this time of crisis that my prayer life improved considerably. It was not so much the words I used, but the passionate way I used them. I was angry, and I told God so. I was sad, and I let Him know it. I was desperate, and you can be sure He was going to get the rough end of it. For the most part it seemed as if I were just talking to myself. There was no response, and certainly no such thing as a gentle voice from heaven bringing comfort to my soul. I did not hear such things as 'This is my beloved son who is having a hard time. Take pity on him!' Day after day, week after week and month after month, for the best part of two years the silence went on and on and on. Not even from my daily Bible readings (which weren't so daily) did I get a 'word from the Lord'. It was an ongoing struggle just for me to believe that He was there at all. I knew all the right things to say to people in my situation – things like 'Trust in the Lord and He will deliver you', 'Be still and know that I am God', 'I will never leave you nor forsake you', 'Put your trust in God' and so on. I can just hear myself mouthing them to anyone in similar circumstances. While they are all true and while they should all bring some encouragement, for my part my mouth was constantly dry and my palms were often sticky from apprehension. My bones literally ached and my heart was jelly in my chest. I often had loose bowel motions because of the stress of it all. I was constantly asking God for answers. After all, doesn't it say in the Bible, 'Ask and it shall be given. Knock and the door shall be opened'? But does this mean that you should hammer and bash at the door of heaven like a man possessed? I believe that you have to *learn* to have the capacity to receive answers and to understand that even an omnipotent God does not always provide all the answers. It has been suggested that often we lose that capacity in our passion for results in this 'quick fix' world. We want solutions and we want them now. We want answers, and we want to know why it was necessary to go through all that suffering. What was the purpose and how could I possibly benefit from it? It simply doesn't help to be told that God's time-clock ticks at a different beat to our own.

Grief does feel like being pulled apart at the extremities. I suppose it has to do with the fact that many of our responses are conditioned, or even habitual. Our expectations for life are, in many cases, due to certain aspects of that life, maybe our husbands or wives, our children, our jobs or our possessions. When we lay them down, or are forced to lay them down, our security system is threatened, if not destroyed. We have forgotten that ultimately our security should be in the One who made us.

In my inner being, I never stopped believing in God. Somehow I just felt as if He had passed me by.

I did not cope by knowing that God would deliver me from hell on earth 'one day'. Nor did it help to realise that next month things might get better – or even next week. I coped by taking life one hour at a time. I did not even give myself the luxury of hoping that tomorrow would be better, for fear that it would not. I dealt with life quite literally as it came. I could not cope with the past because it was gone and to revive it, or relive it, brought too much hurt and only drove me deeper into guilt and despair. I could not cope with tomorrow. For me, to live in the future was to live in fear. I believed that if terror could strike once, it could strike again – lightning can strike twice in the same place. So what was I left with? Just the present. And somehow it makes reasonable sense to live one's life at this point, as 'now' is all the time we have available to us. No wonder Jesus tells us not to be over-concerned about tomorrow. It is helpful to remember that dreading tomorrow is always worse than living today.

So the first thing I did was to take life one day at a time.

The second was to wait on God. It is one of the hardest things in life to do. The waiting seemed interminable.

After our return to England from South Africa in late 1993, God had already provided a home with Mary's mum. Now He also began to provide friends. Martyn and Helen Atkins were just what we needed as a safe haven. It was not too long after we had put our bags down in Devon that we met this unlikely pair, and that meeting became a turning point.

Martyn is a theological academic with a PhD. He is now ensconced in developing post-graduate studies at a theological college. At the time we met he was chaplain at an independent school in North Devon, and he lived right next door. He would call a spade 'an agricultural implement used for the purpose of maintaining the aerobic integrity and nutritional stability of the soil', whereas Helen (a practice nurse) would refer to it as 'sumthin yer dig' oles with'. Both were from Yorkshire (we won't hold that against them) and both were responsible for stripping off the spiritual Band-aids and letting the air do a proper healing job. It was through Martyn (and of course, the headmistress) that I became a history teacher at the school and recovered much of my self-confidence. He was fairly sane, except when his computer went down or one of his children deleted a file containing an essay or document that he had spent hours and hours on. Then we would have to scrape him off the ceiling with a spatula. This spatula often took the form of a visit to the pub in Abbotsham, where the ale would flow and gradually all would seem right with the world again. Martyn was a part-time rock musician who trained as a catering manager so that he could become a Methodist minister. If you can make any sense out of that then you can understand him. But nobody really can!

Helen is a gem, by no means a rough diamond but one of life's real treasures. It takes no effort at all to love her dearly. In the end she became an integral part of Mary's recovery. Things always go wrong for Helen and we would often fall on the floor and cry with laughter at her antics. She never intended these things to happen – they just did. Like the time she fell in the bog when taking the Cubs for an outing. Or the time she screamed and jumped a foot in the air when she caught sight of a slow-worm, mistaking it for an adder. On another occasion she set up a tent in beautiful weather only to be washed out by dawn. She hates creepy things, and on this occasion was most alarmed to discover that, in the deluge, a frog had made its home in her hair. It wasn't just the events that were so amusing, but the way she would describe them. They were a panacea for our own pain, and certainly God's provision for our recovery.

At the same time I had begun to take on preaching appointments in North Devon. There were many churches in need of preachers and I was happy to get back into some form of activity in the Church. It was a strange sensation as, even while I felt estranged from God, I continued to preach about His faithfulness. However, as often happens, one thing led to another and I began to get regular opportunities to preach on Sunday mornings. Mary at this time was filling her day with any opportunity to see it out. She would take computer courses or work in charity shops. Idleness, we both knew, would be the end of us. It is very important to remember that, in circumstances like ours, keeping busy is vital. An unoccupied mind is fertile soil for self-pity to flourish and grow. So, as best as we were able, we tried to keep ourselves active.

It was about April 1994 that I was asked to fill in as a part-time history teacher at Edgehill College, where Martyn was chaplain. It was to be another turning point. I had never considered myself as a teacher even though I had done quite a bit of part-time school teaching while working as a pastor in South Africa. It was still my intention to return to the ministry as soon as an opportunity presented itself. But it never did, and to compound the situation I did not expect to enjoy teaching so much. Enjoy it? I loved it. The kids – well, you can't call seventeen to eighteen-year-olds kids – were great. All those teenagers who were part of the A-level history group in my first twelve months there will never realise how much they helped me to recover. I had lost one seventeen-year-old son in 1993 and now, a year later, I was given dozens to deal with. Kids have that amazing capacity to take your mind off your problems. Let me be quick to say that Richard can never be replaced in my heart; I still grieve over his loss. But suddenly here I was, caught up again in the youthful zest for life that he once had. I still love my son and I look forward to the day when we will meet again. Is that not the great hope of the Christian Church? I dearly love my two girls, Amanda and Catherine, but I also have a special love for my pupils, both past and present, and I think they like me just a little bit as well. And in July 1994, a year almost to the day after my son's death, the headmistress called and asked if I would come on to her staff full time. Martyn was delighted, and off to the Abbotsham pub we went.

Teaching at the college was, without doubt, a major factor

in my recovery. Not only did the headmistress demonstrate remarkable faith in one who had much less faith in himself, but she also gave me the opportunity to use my musical ability once again when she asked me to run the school orchestra. It is, without doubt, the greatest orchestra on earth! Well, the North Devon bit of earth, at any rate.

It was, in many ways, a second chance. But then, as I think about it, I have come to the conclusion that there is no such thing as a second chance. They are all first chances. We must make the best of what we have at the time we have it.

13

Out of the Tunnel

Some of us stumble on foothills
Some of us soar to the stars
Some of us overcome trouble
And some of us live with the scars.

(Source unknown)

Today, as I write, it is Friday 25th July 1997.
The fourth anniversary of Richard's death.

Arriving at my classroom on the first day as a full-time
teacher, I was faced in my very first lesson with a group
of seventeen-year-old girls, who all looked at me with an
expression that said, 'Right, you're the new guy. What are
you going to say to me that is going to make me want to
stay in your class?' All through the summer holiday and
from the moment that I knew that I would be working full
time I had been preparing for this moment.

I had done part-time teaching before and I had preached
hundreds of sermons during my ministry. So I was not too
intimidated by public speaking or giving a lecture. But in my
case it had usually been one-way traffic; there had seldom,
if ever, been interruption or disruption of any kind. That
was about to change.

'History,' I began, stuffing my hands into my pockets and walking among the desks (I too had watched the movie *Dead Poets Society*), 'is probably *the* most boring subject a person can do.' I looked out of the window, deliberately avoiding their gazes. 'I mean, who wants to study a bunch of dead people? Who wants to learn about events that took place ages ago and can have no possible relevance to our lives today?' One or two of the students began to look at each other and raise the odd eyebrow. I turned from the window and spoke to them from the back of the classroom so that they had to twist in their chairs to look at me. 'C'mon, let's get real, only a halfwit would want to take this stuff seriously.' Silence. I measured my steps to the front of the class. Eyes followed. They were now not sure how to take it. 'Why do it?' I half-motioned to Anna sitting by the window. She began to open her mouth. 'It's so-o-o boring,' I repeated. 'I don't even know how I'm gonna teach it. I'll probably be asleep before you.' I paused and peered at them. 'But then, it's not all bad 'cause you are an all-girl class and –' I grinned mischievously and for the first time they got a hint that something was coming, '– and academics and females don't go together, so it doesn't matter if you sleep.' They began to bristle. 'I know,' I said with a superior air of authority, 'I have three females in my house and women should be barefoot, pregnant and in the kitchen.' That did it. There was uproar. Paper was ripped from pads and rolled into projectiles.

'You male chauvinist.' yelled one, whose paper cannon-ball bounced off the blackboard.

'I know,' I laughed. 'But you even throw like a girl. Not straight.' She opened her mouth.

'Don't, Jamie, can't you see he's winding us up?' Zoe

folded her arms and said, 'Anyway, I don't find it boring. If I did I wouldn't be doing it at A level.' Many months later, when the final exam results came out, Zoe was to rush up to me in the corridor outside the head's office and fling her arms around me. 'I got an A, Mr O, I got an A! Isn't it great?!'

But now they stared back at me as I pulled a chair up and sat beside them. 'I know it's not boring. It's what you make of it, like everything else in life.' I paused. 'And I'm not a male chauvinist. I think you are very special people . . . 'cause I once knew a young man who I sort of took for granted. It was only when he left me and went away that I realised how special he was.'

'My mum thinks I'm useless,' muttered one of them. I pretended not to hear the remark.

'History is a window through which we look backward so that we can have a reasonable grasp for the future. If anyone should ignore the past, then they have little prospect of dealing with what tomorrow may throw at them.'

'Like Hitler,' said Lisa.

'Mmm, the list is endless,' I replied, 'but remember that even you, sitting here, are having and will have an effect on the pages of history. I read in *Time* magazine a little while ago that "History is not made by kings or princes, but by ordinary people, doing extraordinary things". It's my job to try and make this subject about dead people come alive for you.'

I then began to outline the syllabus we would be looking at for the rest of the year and gave out some books and some forward reading. As the class began to draw to a close, something magical happened. Without looking up at them I responded to the girl who had told me that she was useless. It was spontaneous – I certainly did not plan it. 'Whatever you have been told in the past that has made you feel insignificant and small, by whoever it was and whenever it was, I want you to know that you *are* special. And I never want to hear you say to me again that you are useless or of no worth. You *are* special and of immense worth. And I will try and do everything to help you succeed. But the key to success is in you. Only you can turn that key.' They stared back at me. It was a special moment. 'A teacher once told me that the only time I would be of any use of anyone was when I donated my body to a hospital.' They laughed. 'That,' I smiled back at them, 'was exactly the reaction of the class. They laughed. But do you know how it made me feel?'

'Like crap,' one of them mused.

'Well, I'm a Christian and I'd be glad if you could watch your language – not so much for my sake, but for yours. But that's exactly how I felt and I don't ever want you to feel like that in this class. The knowledge that you will acquire in this room is one thing, but the belief that you can do something with that knowledge is quite another. I'm going to try and get you to believe that you can. You see, I want you to learn without you even realising that you are doing it.'

I knew we would be able to get along just fine as a group. Master and students and, I hoped, friends. The bell broke the moment and they headed off in all directions.

Edgehill College was established by the Methodist Church in 1884 as an independent (private) all-girls school and is situated on a hill of some sixty acres overlooking the Torridge estuary and the rolling North Devon countryside.

Like many single-sex schools in Britain, it has, in recent years, become co-educational and now caters for children from infants to sixth form. It has quite a cosmopolitan feel, as students from as far afield as Hong Kong, Germany, the United States, the Czech Republic and parts of Africa take advantage of the boarding facilities.

For me, the first two years at Edgehill were the light at the end of a very long and dark tunnel, but not the exit from it. I found myself constantly looking over my shoulder, awaiting a twist in the tunnel that would plunge me back into darkness. Martyn Atkins, the chaplain, always encouraged me not to allow these feelings of insecurity to overcome me, and indeed there was no justification for them. But I suppose the feelings were understandable – many who have endured multiple loss in a short space of time wonder when the next blow will come. I reasoned to myself that as I was relatively inexperienced as a teacher, I might at any time receive a call from the headmistress who would politely inform me that while I had tried my best it was not going to work . . . The call never came and it took me well into my third year to realise that that particular twist to my journey down the tunnel was not likely to happen. Of course, I realise that we have no guarantees of the future. Richard taught me that we are all but a heartbeat from God. So, as I have said elsewhere, we make the best of what we've got at the time we've got it. Even sickbags!

When you are dealing with children you have to be prepared for any eventuality at any time. They have an amazing ability to take your mind off your problems and suck you into their own. No one's problems are larger than a teenager's – no one's. World War III may be about to occur, but should a teenager break out in acne or a friend go off with someone else, the mind boggles. Even naming a bottle-green cello case Myrtle, because it looks like a turtle, takes on special significance.

But let me not minimise some of the very real problems that teenagers face today. They are legion. There are problems at school and at home; problems with pressures that have intensified over the years; expectations, hopes and dreams; competition in exams and in places for university; the difficulty in finding work when they leave school – the list is endless. But it is the little problems that seem so big that are amusing. Like our trips to London.

Whenever we take students to London we use either a school mini-bus or a coach, depending on the numbers. Because Bideford is just over four hours' drive from London, departure is always at some God-forsaken hour of the morning. Packed lunches are stowed in the belly of the bus and the medical box, containing the dreaded sickbags, is up front with the teachers.

'Clive, you can be in charge of sickbags,' said Gina as we prepared to take a group to the Houses of Parliament, 'I can't stand the smell.'

'Fine with me,' I replied recklessly, 'doesn't bother me in the slightest. Anyway, this bunch are sixth-formers. They should be fine.' Gina looked at me. 'What does she know that I don't?' I thought to myself, as sweets, packets of crisps, cans of Coke and Sony Walkmans were passed back and forth behind us.

We had only been on the road for about an hour.

'Mrs Crouch, Cathy's going to be sick!'

'Too much chocolate too early in the morning,' Gina

muttered to me. 'Your first case.' With that she handed me the sickbags.

'Quick, quick,' shouted a desperate child fanning her cheek with her splayed fingers. And she wasn't the sick one. I thrust the bag towards the stricken pupil.

'Whoossh' – out it came. Some into the bag. Most on to the seat in front of her. Crisps, chocolate and Coke. It dripped like treacle to the floor.

'Oohh! Gross!' cried Charlotte. A chorus of supportive friends withdrew as if the poor girl was a leper. But the die was cast. Kelly, Katie and Emma began to succumb. The plague spread as the odour wafted up and down the aisle. One by one the number of unused sickbags grew less. I was becoming frantic. Gina Crouch and Mary Hayes, my faithful, loyal and helpful colleagues, busied themselves reading their newspapers, all the while chuckling to themselves. Mercifully we put into a service point on the M5. The way those pupils evacuated the bus would make one think that there was a brood of vipers on board.

Richard, our driver, smiled at me. ''Ere, Cloive,' he said in the rich melodious tones of the Devonian, 'you've got a better stummik than oi 'ave,' and handed me a mop as he hotfooted it to join Mary and Gina at coffee. We still had another two and a half hours ahead of us, as well as the four-hour return trip to look forward to.

I still take bus trips, and I still handle the sickbags even though, in reality, they are hardly ever used. I'm told, and rumour has it, that I'm good at it.

It bears repeating that the problems teenagers face are real, complex and all-embracing. The scars that some of them face will stay with them all their lives. Future plans and expectations will often be made on the memory of childhood experience, and two of the greatest forces that will overtake and possess the teens are hormones and society. These two factors play an enormous role in their lives.

The fact that hormones affect the body is well documented, and the obvious fact of physical change is clear for all to see. But these hormones which change the body also affect the brain. How else can we explain why a happy, contented, co-operative twelve-year-old suddenly becomes an argumentative, sullen, angry and rebellious thirteen-year-old? It is interesting to note that some of these mood swings are not unlike the emotional changes that occur when some men and women reach the so-called mid-life crisis – the time when hormones are supposed to kick *out*. Just as adults need and expect everyone to be patient until they pass the crisis years, so teenagers should receive the same patience. They go through a time of terrific insecurity as they face an uncertain future, and their parents need to ride it out with them until the storm passes and they get their feet underneath themselves again.

The social factor then combines with the horror of hormones to create havoc during adolescence. I find myself in conflict with these forces on a daily basis. They have indeed helped me to emerge from the tunnel of despair which my family and I entered late in 1992. They have helped me in the completely selfish way in which teenagers allow their problems to dominate both their lives and the lives of everyone they encounter. In becoming involved I was able to refocus, to get another perspective. In other words, they forced me, albeit unwittingly, to stop looking at my own problems and to look at other people's.

Society puts terrific pressures on our kids. I will never forget hearing about a vulnerable girl called Lisa. At fifteen, she was asked to perform a modern dance during a school concert. She was one of those kids whose physical development had been slow, and she had been on the receiving end of some unkind comments about her physique. As she spun about the stage the unthinkable happened. The top of her skimpy blouse became undone and flew off her body during a fierce turn. The assembled students roared as the terrified girl was left frantically trying to cover herself with her hands. In tears she fled from the stage. Worse was to follow. She was never allowed to forget the incident as almost daily she lived with the taunts.

Little can be worse for a teenager. Indeed, it would be bad enough for an adult. An embarrassment of this size could easily take away the desire to live, and certainly hundreds of our precious teens are killing themselves every year because they simply cannot cope with society's pressures. What then is to be done for them? The frustration of being not quite a child and not yet an adult, the fear of failure, the feeling of not being acceptable to others or to oneself, all these play their part in the life of the modern teenager. And for me, being flung from a time of disorder, confusion and hurt into this cauldron of emotion, it was inevitably a panacea for my own pain. I couldn't help but love these kids, with their pimples and their problems. For I have found:

When children live with tolerance and fair treatment,
   They learn to be patient and fair with others.
When children live with encouragement,
   They learn to be confident and secure.
When children live with praise and compliments,

They learn appreciation.
When children live with fairness,
   They learn the meaning of justice.
When children live with security,
   They learn to have faith.
When children live with approval,
   They learn to like themselves.
When children live with unconditional acceptance,
   They learn to find love in God and the world.
(Dorothy Law Nolte, *Children Learn What They Live*)

It is fair to say that it was in trying to deal with these children, in seeing them sob through their heartaches and yell through their tantrums, that I found myself emerging from my long, dark journey. But even though I had settled down in North Devon for over three years, it took a long letter from one teenage girl to finally bring me out of the tunnel. This story is integral in my recovery.

Louise had suffered a teenage nightmare – anorexia nervosa. Hormones and the expectations of a teenage society, compounded by the fact that her body was wasting, drove her into despair. She wrote to me: 'I lost all my self-respect and began hating myself intensely. I felt I was an utter failure.' Whenever Louise felt a failure, even in so small a way as losing a point at tennis, she would hit herself to inflict pain and then blame her 'stupid body'. She said, 'I wanted to be something I wasn't – I hated Louise.' I know there are countless numbers of teens who have felt as she did. To make matters worse, she would compare herself to other members of her family whom she perceived as successful and would then curl up in their shadow.

139

When I first met Louise, I did not see her as large, or even remotely fat. To me she seemed a normal, well-adjusted, beautiful sixteen-year-old. However, it was a chance comment from an uncaring teenage boy that coloured her view of her size. 'Losing weight then became my life. I shut out everything else. It possessed everything I did and needed.' She embarked upon a protracted course of self-mutilation. Day and night she would exercise in secret, denying herself nourishment in an attempt to lose weight, and in so doing entered a very dark tunnel which seemed to have no end. It was at first a very lonely and frightening experience, as all her fears and longings were kept to herself. 'I did not want to be the same sort of person again. Not only did I set about changing my body shape, but my personality began to alter. I became a control freak.'

I can completely identify with Louise in this regard. After Richard's death and after my loss of ministry, I did not want to be the same person again. I don't really know what I wanted to be, so long as it was anyone else but me. This, however, is foolhardy, because we are as God made us. The Bible says quite clearly: 'Before I formed you in the womb I knew you' (Jer. 1:5) and 'For you created my inmost being; you knit me together in my mother's womb' (Ps. 139:13). It is a beautiful picture, an astounding claim for creation that our modern-day science forces us to repudiate. It is so sad that in a society that has all but lost its perspective on God we should want to change His handiwork because we are dissatisfied with it. But this is a market-driven phenomenon. It is an advertising gimmick, which makes us dissatisfied with what we've got and what we are. It says we must be young, beautiful, successful and wealthy – if not, we are losers. Thank God He doesn't see it that way. But you don't know that when you are in the tunnel.

Louise became wrapped up in herself.

> After battling against the cold, which was unbearable; the obsessional exercise; school . . . I knew I was killing myself but I just could not fight it and at the same time I neglected any help . . . I was in my own private hell and wouldn't let anyone else enter into it. Then one night, reality sank in. I was losing $4^1/_2$ lb a week and by this time I was under six stone. I had just finished a gruelling exercise routine and collapsed. I could feel my heart pounding, straining irregularly in my puny, mutilated child's body. I thought that I was going to die. I asked for help and the next day I was in hospital.

It was here that a new battle ensued. Gripped with guilt and remorse for what she thought she had put her family through, Louise tried to get better for their sakes, not her own. She couldn't. And she didn't know why.

There were times when I too felt I had completely failed my family. The decision that I took to resign, the decision I took to return to England, all contributed to a downward spiral and the loss of a child. How can a man carry such a burden? I tried to make amends but I couldn't and I didn't know why. When Louise shared her helplessness with me, a number of factors slotted into place in my own mind and we were able to help each other. The end of the tunnel started to come into view for both of us.

At first she resented my visits to the hospital, thinking that I just wanted to interfere and had no understanding of what she was going through. Even here she had tried to beat the system by cheating on her diet. But in her letter she said, 'Despite our situations being very different, our feelings [of helplessness] were very similar.' It was a visit late one Sunday evening, when I dropped in unexpectedly, that proved significant. Before knocking and pushing open the door, I paused and looked through the little window. Louise was sitting on her bed alone in her ward, leafing through a teenage magazine. She looked so small and frail that my heart nearly broke. 'I've lost one child,' I thought to myself as I stood in the corridor. 'God, I don't want to lose this one. I don't know if I could bear it.' And she wasn't even my own. I pushed the door open.

'Hi, gorgeous. How are you doing?' She didn't look up and I dropped into a chair and began to eat the sweets that lay on the bedside table.

'Not too good.' Her voice was very faint. She had been in hospital for nearly fourteen weeks. 'I'm so tired and so lonely and I'll never get better.' She kept her head down to hide the tears. 'I was told that I've gone backward because I've lost a few pounds this week. I'll never get out of this place.' It was as if something had gripped my throat; I was unable to speak. I put the sweets down and moved beside the stricken child. We had shared quite a bit of our respective stories with each other and a bond of trust had developed. A cold fury boiled inside me. 'How could anyone say such a thing?' I thought to myself. Despite their great learning, all those degrees and diplomas that they can paper their walls with, there are a few in the medical profession who still have much to learn about 'beside manner' – about the giving of hope.

'You haven't gone backward,' I said, 'and you mustn't

see it as such.' Louise lifted her head. 'You've just lost some weight this week. If you see it as going backward then you'll never get out of the tunnel. Going backward means that you are not going forward. And you *are* going forward.' Louise looked puzzled and blew her nose. 'View it as a twist in the tunnel, a turn where you have lost sight of the end of it. But not backward, You are still going forward and we will see the light again. Soon.'

I put my arms about her and prayed aloud. 'God, make Louise better and get her out of this place.' I remember the words clearly.

She wrote,

> You made me feel that you were on my side and that you brought God with you. You made me realise that I was never facing any of the journey alone no matter what I did. Even if I blamed Him, God would not give up on me and would understand. When you touched my head and asked God for help I immediately felt strong, like I had the greatest thing on my side. God's presence made me feel ready to take on anorexia, and conquer it.

'God's presence made me feel ready to take it on and conquer it.' What a profound statement from a teenager. I had not always felt God's presence, but like Louise I knew He had not deserted me.

Louise is out of hospital now. She was sent home shortly after our prayer. She still feels scared and says, 'I'm not at the end of the tunnel yet and at times I think I'm going backward, but I know I'm not.' A sort of fear mixed with faith. Is that not the story of us all?

'Every day,' Louise says, 'I get that bit closer to the end than I was yesterday.'

To see her now is to see a radiant young woman. No, her battle is not yet over, and neither is mine. She faced her fears head on and took some scars and some bruising along the way, but with the love of her family and her friends around her, she can write a chapter of courage and triumph in her life. What a tribute to her character.

14

Vengeance is a Bitter Pill

*We take captive every thought to make it obedient
to Christ.*

(2 Cor. 10:5b)

I've always been interested in trees. As a child I liked to
climb them and as I grew older I appreciated the shapes
they made and the shade they provided. I can remember
one tree I could see from my bedroom window; its foliage
looked like the face of an old man with a long nose looking
up into the sky. I used to greet him most days and whenever
I had to spend time in bed I would tell him what was wrong.
I remember how his features would move and shift when
the breeze pulled at him. Sometimes, when the wind was
strong, he would become unrecognisable, and I thought he
was gone for ever, as if it were impossible for the tree to
regain its original shape. But it always did, and when the
wind had died away there he was again, my man in the tree.
Finally when I moved away from that house, I can remember
looking at him for the last time, and noticing that a bough
had broken off where his eyebrow had been. He had lost
his distinctive appearance and if I were to go back to that
house today, I doubt if I would find him again.

One autumn during half-term on the Yorkshire Dales, I

remember being particularly impressed with certain trees. The colours of the falling leaves were breathtaking – vast avenues of red and brown, gold and yellow, that no human hand could recreate.

One particular day in April 1996 trees took on a new perspective for me, especially from the vantage point I was given. I was on my back, looking straight up at them. Now this may not seem all that strange: people often lie down on the grass and look at the trees above them and the sky beyond. Usually, though, they do so by choice. This was not the case with me. I lay on my back with my legs tangled up in the frame of an ancient bicycle that my brother-in-law had lent me so that I could get some exercise along the Tarka Trail, a converted railway track in North Devon. A Robertson's Golly transfer, which John, my strange Golly-collecting brother-in-law, had thoughtfully stuck on to the bike, stared back at me. In my state of punctured pride, I thought I saw it wink.

I am not a man given to using strong language of any sort. Had I been hurt I might have said, 'Damn it!' or something to that effect. But I wasn't, and as a spinning wheel squeaked to a halt, I muttered my favourite expletive, 'Bottom!'

The young lady who had caused me to veer off the track and career into the undergrowth had vanished into the distance. Well, when I say that she had caused me to crash, it is possible that she had no idea she had done so. She didn't actually collide with me – in fact she hadn't even touched me as we passed each other going in opposite directions. She just did what most travellers do when passing on the Tarka Trail, whether on foot or cycle. She smiled and said, 'Hello'. Foolishly, I glanced over my shoulder as she passed, for a final glimpse of her beautiful flowing auburn hair and curvaceous shape, and lost control of my feeble old bike.

The birds that had flown screeching in fright during my headlong charge had now resettled, and their song once again mingled with the bubbling of the upper reaches of the Torridge as it splashed over the weir at Weare Giffard on its way to the sea below Bideford. As I listened to them I thought how much like the river they sounded, a sort of blending of nature.

There I lay, not too uncomfortable, surrounded by moss and fern and the dank smell of rotting tree bark and leaves. It was an unlikely setting for the start of such a project as writing a book. For some time I had been contemplating chronicling the feelings and emotions that had led me to this point in my life. They had been very strong emotions, and they were emotions that had led to feelings of guilt, because, as a clergyman, I had always been taught – and, indeed, had myself taught – that for Christians it was wrong to feel anger and to want harm to come to those who had hurt me or my family. The plain fact of the matter was that I did feel these emotions. And I felt them acutely. Now as I lay beneath the trees I resolved to get on with the task of putting them down on paper.

The real purpose of my scribblings was to demonstrate how utterly fallible Christians are, whether they stand in lofty pulpits or whether they sit in humble pews; how utterly human they are; and, thank God, to discover that it is possible to be a Christian despite being imperfect.

How was I to begin to describe the sensations, the feelings

and passions that were boiling, pent up and in some cases still unresolved? I didn't know – maybe I would never be able to convey then fully. I disentangled my legs from John's bike and continued my way along the Tarka Trail to the railway bridge that spanned the river. As I looked at the ribbon of water as it disappeared into the trees, nodding to the waving boatman who passed beneath me, I knew that there are many who feel just as I did. Thoughts began to fill my mind.

How did Cain feel before he slew his brother Abel? What was on Samson's mind before he pushed apart the supports of that pagan temple, causing his own death and that of his enemies? What passion induced the disciple Peter as his sword sliced off the ear of a soldier who laid rough hands on his Lord? Or me, as I pondered the hurts of the past few years? Or countless men and women who through the ages have for personal, private, political or professional reasons desired to take their pound of flesh, and take it to their cost? For, although many may claim it to be so, revenge is not sweet. I felt vengeful, I was angry, but, thank God, I did nothing about those emotions. I really believed that in taking any action I would be creating a burden that I would not be able to bear. And God knows, Mary, Amanda, Catherine and I had borne enough pain.

I had just been reading a book about the last woman to be executed in England, Ruth Ellis, who would no doubt agree (if she could) that revenge is not sweet. In a fit of jealous rage she sought, stalked and shot her drunken, philandering and cheating lover, David Blakely. I was interested in the case as in 1984, in Cape Town, I had met one of the officials who had attended her execution at Holloway prison in 1955.

In a clear-cut case of wilful murder she offered no substantial defence and refused to ask for clemency as a downtrodden mistress. She made little of his beatings, saying, 'He only used his fists and hands, but I bruise very easily.' With all her pain, passion and fury spent, Ruth Ellis wanted to die for murdering her lover. Reading her story, I had felt sadness at the sheer waste of two lives caused through her unchecked passions.

In cross-examination only one question was asked by the prosecutor: 'Mrs Ellis, when you fired that revolver at close range into the body of David Blakely, what did you intend to do?'

'It is obvious,' she replied, sealing her fate, 'that when I shot him I intended to kill him.' After only twenty-three minutes of deliberation, the jury found her guilty of murder.

On 13th July 1955, Ruth Ellis wrote a last note to a friend from the condemned cell. 'The time is 7 a.m. – everyone is simply wonderful in Holloway. This is just to console my family with the thought that I did not change my way of thinking at the last moment. Or break my promise to David's mother.' In an earlier note Ruth had asked forgiveness and written, 'I shall die loving your son.'

Perhaps she did. Just before 9.00 a.m. a grim procession of officials entered her cell and told her that the time had come. After thankfully accepting a large glass of brandy she walked calmly to the execution room, where Albert Pierrepoint discharged his grisly duty. In her case, most graphically illustrated, the wages of sin was indeed death.

For his part in the day's events Pierrepoint received a fee of fifteen guineas plus expenses. He then left Holloway prison and needed police protection from the

jeering, storming mob that had besieged it. He returned
to his 'other job' as a publican at the Rose and Crown
at Hoole, near Preston. There he resolved to give up the
macabre post, occupied by his father and uncle before him.
All three had been listed by the Home Office as 'professional
executioners'. When his decision became known, it was
supposed that something particularly gruesome had taken
place in the death chamber. In fact nothing of the sort
had happened. Pierrepoint had resigned because of his
own conscience. He questioned if hanging really did deter
murder and came to the conclusion that it did not. 'Ruth
Ellis was the bravest woman I ever hanged and nothing
untoward happened that terrible day.' He went on to
say that capital punishment achieved nothing except the
revenge of society.

Perhaps these were strange thoughts for a beautiful setting
such as rural North Devon, but they filled my mind as my
bike clanked along the path. What was it that drove Ruth
Ellis to want to get even? Why is it so important to get
your own back even if there is no longer any risk to your
person or property? Why is it so difficult for so many of
us to let bygones be bygones? Why is it so important for
society at large to impose its ever-changing standards of
ethics and morality, even when most of us, who sit in
judgment on others, have never been affected other than
by what we have read in the papers? Why is it that books
and films on betrayal, lust, anger, intrigue, violence and
revenge attract our attention more than any other sort?
The only answer to these questions is that this makes up
base human nature.

Indeed, as I can inflict great harm on others as well

as myself even without realising it, I have need of God's restraint and his law. At the same time, I also have a need to be protected from others, for many would take what I possess for want of it themselves. For this I have the restraint of the state, with its laws and protection. Without the power of the state, anyone who is stronger than I am can take from me whatever they please. The law holds no terror and is nothing more than a statement on a piece of paper if it is not imposed, and what is rightfully mine can become anyone's by force. It is the law of the jungle – the concrete jungle. It says what is yours by rights and justice is yours only as long as you (or someone else) can protect it. In most cases all that is left for the victim is the strong desire for revenge. In some, this desire leads to action.

In the case of holding on to God's law, the restraints of conscience can protect us from desires that may bring us harm, and are summed up in the principles of the Ten Commandments: love your God and love your neighbour. While this might protect me from wrongful actions, it does not protect me from my emotions. When I allowed myself to think about the events that had brought me from South Africa to England, inwardly I seethed. There were times when I was quite literally taken captive by these thoughts. They occupied my waking moments and ruined my day. I had to master them, or they would certainly master me. I had to practise and exercise quite determinedly to take my mind off the past. I had to 'take captive every thought and make it obedient to Christ'. I tried to do this by reading, praying, writing, and so on. Sometimes I was successful. Often I failed, and found myself wallowing in the past and all its ills. I also found that the more I practised 'captive thinking', the more positive I became and the better I got at it. I suppose it's a bit like most things in life: the more you practise, the better you get.

There is nothing like the things of this world to bring one back to the reality of it. Riding my bike along the Tarka Trail had suddenly become more difficult – the front tyre had become flat! It was probably the result of my headlong flight into the foliage. I continued the rest of my journey home, muttering.

15

Fathers and Sons – The Living Years

*We must say the words that must be spoken
before they are lost for ever.*

(Anon.)

One of the last moments I spent in Cape Town was on a
large rock, alone, one late November evening, silhouetted
against the setting sun on a windswept beach where a few
months before we had scattered the ashes of my only son.
The shore was deserted and the sky was a tapestry of
colour. It was cold and I shivered in the wind, but I sat
on the rock for some hours, until it was quite dark. This
was where Richard had spent time with his friends, where
we had spent time, father and son, so many years before,
playing together in the sand. Now there was just the spray
of the sea, and the memory.

I will not have another chance with him, this son of mine,
so what do I do with the regrets I have for time and promises
unfulfilled? Times when I criticised him unfairly and hurt
him unduly, when I failed to affirm my love for him or
neglected to play sport with him because like many parents,
if not most, I found the time to be with others but not
him. What do I do with this burden of guilt and regret?

If he were alive I could say I was sorry and make amends. But he is not, and I shall only see him again in the life to come. What can I do with the pain of remorse for having let him down, let alone the pain of having lost him?

Jesus said, 'Come unto me, all of you who are burdened, and I will give you rest.' This is not a promise I can ever take lightly. God, I know, forgives. I have no doubt of this one fact. But between Richard and me there still remain some unresolved matters, matters that in this life can never be put right. My hurt remains, not just the hurt of loss but the hurt of knowing that I let him down. So I ask God to pass on a message to my son who is in the presence of his Saviour. The prayer is simple and honest. 'Tell Ricky that I miss him, that I love him and that I'm sorry I messed up so much while I was his dad.' Then I leave it with my Dad, who doesn't mess up.

For me to live in the past, telling myself how bad I was and how much I screwed up, results only in guilt, so I have to put it behind me and start again, looking after and loving all I meet; quite naturally, this includes my family, my professional colleagues and my students. Not just for Richard's sake, not just for his memory, but for God's sake. If I could turn back the clock, just to see his face again, I would, but of course I can't. I would give away all I have to bring him back to us, but that is impossible. I would even knowingly go through all the pain of the last few years – yes, again – fully understanding that we would one day part the way we did, just to hold him again for an instant. For it *is* true that it is better to have loved and lost than never to have loved at all.

As I sat on that lonely sea-shore that cold November evening, T.S. Eliot's poem, *Four Quartets*, came to mind.

He writes that 'we must be still and still moving forward into another intensity', seeking 'a deeper communion', even though the darkness is cold, empty and desolate. As the waves crash and cry and the winds howl over the vast waters, Eliot makes the claim that 'in my end is my beginning'. And although, at times, it felt as if Richard's death were the end for me, I knew that with God's patient help it was in fact my beginning.

I have good memories of my own father who, at sixty-three, died of lung cancer when I was thirty-one and Richard was four. We had spent my early years, until I suppose I was about fourteen or fifteen, getting along just fine. It seemed to me that my parents enjoyed a reasonably average marriage. They had their share of arguments, but there was never any violence and I never once heard them talk of divorce. Certainly, I never felt insecure. My mother never had to go out to work as my father's printing business was fairly successful, but the price was that he was kept busy building it up. So when I say I enjoyed a good relationship with my father, it was in part to do with the fact that we spent little time together as father and son, except, of course, for holidays. Even on weekends he would spend almost every Saturday playing golf and I had little one-to-one time with him. However, I vividly remember a riotous game of football in the back garden with a tennis ball; I remember it so clearly because it was rare.

A tennis ball is not the easiest piece of equipment to play soccer with, except of course for the very agile. My father was good at music and art (he played the piano and his oil paintings were more than competent), and he played a good game of golf off a fifteen handicap, but when it came to using his feet he was rather useless. Perhaps that is why he often refused my pressing invitations to play soccer. That evening in the back garden, after a severe pounding from his twelve-year-old son, he vigorously aimed a right foot at the tiny object. I have this picture in my mind of legs and arm disappearing into a rose bush, whose unforgiving thorns did little to improve my English vocabulary. To my howls of derision and delight, he staggered defeated from the field of play to pour himself a large whisky.

He did, however, support my own sporting endeavours and attended many of my school and club team games. We sometimes went to the movies together and we enjoyed the little time we did have, but any physical contact between us, like hugging, was altogether out of the question. I don't remember ever kissing him. It just wasn't done.

It wasn't too long ago that I discovered the horrifying statistic that the average United States father spends only forty-five seconds a day in face-to-face contact with his son. *Forty-five seconds!* It is almost unbelievable! The statistic in Britain is somewhat better and improving every year, but is still far short of what it ought to be.

Let us imagine a typical household, anywhere in Britain, first thing in the morning. Let us also assume that in this particular household the parents are not separated or divorced and the father has not left for work before the children leave for school. As you can see, the field has narrowed considerably. Breakfast is served at the table in the kitchen (again, a narrowing of the field).

The father is seated at the table, neatly dressed, buttering some toast and reading the morning paper. A fifteen-year-old lad with sleepy eyes, unkempt hair and scruffy school clothes crashes through the door, switches on the small portable telly, flings open the door of the fridge, reaches for the milk and slops it into a bowl filled to the brim with cornflakes. The bowl is now so full that to put a spoon into it would result in spilling some of its contents on to the table. Not a word has passed between the two as the bemused father peers at his offspring over the top of his reading glasses. He has learnt by experience that this is not a time to be jovial or frivolous.

'Morning, son.'

'Mmmfgrnt.'

'Anything planned for today? Anything interesting happening?' The father is a patient man.

'Nmmfgrnt.' The lad chomps away and studies the cornflakes box as if it were a map to buried treasure. The father sighs and employs the old tried, tested and bound-to-get-a-response technique.

'Do try to brush your hair and clean your shoes before you go out, son.'

'Shtop pficking on me!' A slight spluttering of cornflakes as the mouth empties itself of its contents. 'You are always picking on me.' The father opens his mouth as if to say something but reaches for his car keys instead.

'See you later tonight, and don't forget the dog.'

The entire conversation has lasted less than a minute and is fairly typical. I know that there are homes where father and son spend hours in close, vibrant conversation. But these, sadly, are not the norm. It has been recorded that British children watch an average of three hours of television a day. In the USA it is even longer. Less than a minute versus three hours. It must pose the question ... Who is teaching the kids?

The breakfast incident, recorded above, was almost

identical to a conversation that my father had with his only son (except for the television: there was no TV in South Africa when I was a child) and was fairly typical of several breakfast sessions that I had with my only son. How I wish that I could turn the clock back now, in both cases.

I turned out a bit like my father and my son turned out a bit like me. The question that this raises is: is that what we want for each other? What could I have done to make it different?

I have to live with the knowledge that there is nothing further I can teach Richard, nothing I can share with him. Not in these living years. I can no longer be a hero to him.

It may seem a strange thought for parents to consider themselves heroes to their children. Teenage heroes usually take the form of an Eric Cantona or a Michael Jackson or a Tom Cruise. How do parents compete with people like that? Well, I believe that parents can. This is a lesson that Richard taught me. He did it by writing something on little scraps of paper which I found in a little box along with other bits of writing early in 1997, nearly four years after his death.

Some years ago a Radio One disc jockey did a survey of over three hundred teenagers. He asked them to define a hero and say who their favourite hero was. Most definitions were 'someone who is cool'. A few said someone who was brave. Not a single teenager said, 'my mum or dad'. I'm not sure that equating a well-known entertainer with the word 'hero' does the *Longman Family Dictionary* any justice at all. 'Hero: n a. A mythological or legendary figure endowed with great strength or ability. b. An illustrious warrior. c. A person admired for noble achievements and qualities.' I have a problem with making a soccer star or a heavyweight boxer a hero just because they are good with a football or a pair of boxing gloves. All too often these 'heroes' have gone home and beaten up their wives or kids or got drunk at a party and then been convicted of rape – hardly role models for our kids. And believe me, teenagers are not fooled for long. As someone once said: 'You can con a con; you can fool a fool; but you can't kid a kid.' Not for long, at any rate.

So how do we define the term 'hero'? I believe it ought to be 'someone that I would want to be like'. A hero is not much of a hero if you don't want to emulate him or her. To my mind, a hero is not just someone who is good at an activity, like singing or performing on the sports field. Nor are they just talk. Their walk and their manner bear out who and what they are. They are prepared to give and to sacrifice their time to make their values come alive, especially to those with whom they are closest, their family. It is in this area that parents can offer so much, but in fact contribute so little. And the reason? Time. There is always tomorrow. We'll do it tomorrow. We've all heard it; we've all said it. Tomorrow. I can hear myself say it over and over again to my children: 'Let's go tomorrow.' There were times when we did, but there were many times when we didn't.

In the gospel of Luke, Jesus tells a story that had a lot to say about role models, both good and bad. He told of the dangers of a blind man leading another blind man, of how the one could lead the other into a ditch. He also told us that a pupil is not above his master; only after he has been fully trained, will he be like his teacher (Luke 6:39–40). Here is the real point of being a role model to our children. It is not because we want to be liked or respected or loved, nice as these things are. 'You want to be a hero to your kids in order to equip them to live full and abundant lives in a hurting, hostile and needy world.' (J. McDowell and D. Day in *How to be a Hero to your Kids*.)

Any reasonable parent wants his children to say no to drugs, no to alcohol, no to premarital sex and all the other pressures that are placed upon them by a society which in reality doesn't care for them as much as parents do. If that is true, then the role model must begin at home, *now*, today, no matter what their age. Parents must work at being heroes, and the more they do so the more their children will listen to them and live by their values.

If I were to paraphrase the Luke 6 passage, it would be something like this: 'Children are not above their parents, but all children, after they are nurtured, will be like their parents.' Frightening, isn't it?

Earlier, I mentioned a lesson that my son had given me. It wasn't so much a lesson, more an 'arm about the shoulder'. I had been reliving some of the moments we spent together. Most of it was pleasant, but much of it was self-recrimination. It was a sort of 'if only' situation; as has already been said, you never know what you've got until you've lost it. The same is true for lost parents and certainly for lost children. How I wish I had . . . etc., etc. Then, early in 1997, I happened upon an old wooden box, about the size of a large dictionary. It had been placed to one side along with others which had not

been opened since we had packed up our home in Cape
Town some four years before. It may sound incredible,
but it has taken Mary and me over four years to resettle
and open the last of our boxes now that we have finally
bought a little cottage in Abbotsham. The little wooden
box contained some scraps of paper that our children had
written on. They were messages to me, written during a
time when I was away from home for about six weeks on
church business. I had recently told God in prayer that
I was sorry that I had been such a rubbish father to the
wonderful children that He had given me to take care of
and now, as I sat alone in the garage of our new house
surrounded by memories, three tiny pieces of paper fell
out of the box. They had been written by Richard several
years before.

'Dear Dad, even if you gave me 10,000 spankings, I still
think you're my best bud. Love Richard.' And 'Even if you
did not have money to buy us eneything, I think you're just
great. Love Richard.' Thank you, God, for that. Maybe I
wasn't such a bad dad after all.

Boxes like this will of course contain such surprises. In
this case it was all the more painful as he had helped
pack the boxes himself. His things, awaiting his arrival in
England, all packed before 25th July 1993. There was a box
sealed with half a roll of sticky tape with instructions that it
should not be opened by anyone. It contained letters from
girlfriends, school commendations and reports, newspaper
cuttings. His things, important to him. In another box I
found his tennis racquet, the one he had saved up to buy
from a friend, a high-quality 'Prince' with the sweat stains
from his palms still on the handle. Now, in North Devon,
I sat on a cardboard box and remembered the many times,

the not enough times, we had played together. The living years. The not enough years.

I said that there were three scraps of paper. The third one simply said, 'I'm proud to have you for a dad.' Thank you, God, for that.

16

Back from the Brink?

*Do not be deceived: God cannot be mocked. A
man reaps what he sows.*

(Gal. 6:7)

I have often been asked if it is ever my intention to return
to Cape Town. One thing I have certainly learned is never
to say never. I do not say that as a meaningless cliché; I
really mean it. I have said it myself, and have heard others
say of themselves, that I would *never* do this or that, and
been found doing just this or that, or that I would *never*
get over the hurts of the past. Well, in my case, maybe I
haven't got *over* them, but I have got *on* with them, and
so have others who make the choice to go forward. As
for returning to South Africa, the answer is that I don't
know. I have no plans to. Not because I don't want to but
because, with Mary, I've started again. Torn roots have
been replanted. We will have to see what sort of flower
the new plant produces.

Now, in late 1997, I have become increasingly alarmed at
letters from my family and some friends who express their
concern at rising violence and crime. Without exception
these letters all contain both hope and despair. They tell of

many incidents which, far from being isolated, are becoming commonplace: robberies at knife-point and gun-point in broad daylight, car hijackings at busy intersections, and, on one occasion, a brutal murder in full view of the police. I am well aware that these stories could occur at any place and at any time, but as post-apartheid South Africa holds a special place in my heart, it is of real concern to me.

It is a terrifying illustration of how law and order can be broken down, as victims of rampant crime seek justice where a beleaguered police force have become almost impotent. In some places, vengeance has all but replaced justice as groups seek out and 'punish' the perpetrators of evil. In one case reported to me, a man suspected of dealing in drugs was dragged from his car, shot, set on fire and then allowed to die a horrifying death, all in full view of the media, who recorded it on film, and the police, who stood by and watched. This is one account among many of ongoing crime.

None are immune, as rich and poor, black and white now endure the terror of lawlessness. In an article recently, the London *Daily Mail* reported the attempted robbery of a famous Springbok rugby player's car. It went on to quote the player as stating that he might now seek to play his sport elsewhere in the world as he feared for the safety of himself and his wife, and for the future of his as yet unborn children.

Education too has been at risk, despite the official line. Matric exam papers have been leaked and put up for sale, university places are no longer acquired on the basis of ability, and even degrees are offered for the right price. Not too long ago I received the sad account of a friend who told of disillusioned colleagues leaving the country to seek university teaching posts elsewhere. The fate of universities has enormous symbolic as well as practical significance to the population of South Africa. Let us not forget it was a professor trained at the University of Cape Town who performed the world's first heart transplant. At the same time, we should be painfully aware that African nationalism has devastated all universities north of the Limpopo river, without exception.

There are few, if any, who did not rejoice over the peaceful transition to majority rule in South Africa. It was long, long overdue. And there are many who still live in hope of this 'Rainbow Nation' becoming a shining example of democracy. I am one of them. But it is true that during the period 1995–6 some three to four thousand Whites left the country almost every month and the tide showed little sign of abating in 1997. For the most part, they were the academic/management component of society. Were they rats leaving a sinking ship? Did they see the writing on the wall? What about those who cannot leave, the ones who do not have another passport or the resources to pack up and start again? Must they stand helplessly by and watch their currency devalue almost daily? In 1996 alone the South African rand fell over 30 per cent against the US dollar. The population must let the trappings of colonialism disappear in the sands of time as South Africa reverts to Africa itself. Its many and diverse cultures must blend and mingle, but this is uncomfortable and frightening. The long-awaited and feared bloodbath, thankfully, did not materialise. The patience and tolerance of the black population in general, who have suffered for so long, was astounding, to say the least. Sadly, many pre-1994 election promises have not yet been addressed and unless South Africa can sustain the unlikely annual growth rate of 6 per cent, they will not. Black, white, Asian and coloured will have to endure a time of unprecedented inconvenience as the scales are reset.

A much discussed subject is what might be called the 'post-Mandela phenomenon'. Who will hold the delicate fabric together when Nelson Mandela steps from the stage in the next few short years? His acceptance by all sectors of the population has been remarkable. But there are too many trouble-makers in the wings, not least his bitter and estranged ex-wife.

What has happened to the euphoria of the election and independence? What has happened to Desmond Tutu's 'Rainbow Nation'? What of the Truth and Reconciliation Commission, whose function was to discover the horrors performed during the apartheid years from the very lips of the perpetrators? The noble purpose of these findings was to ascertain the truth so as to offer forgiveness and pardon for political crime. I have been given to understand that those who brought about my son's death have been offered the possibility of a full pardon because of the political nature of their actions, even though Nelson Mandela had been free for some time, the ANC and PAC had been unbanned and a date for full democratic elections had been set. As I write, I await the outcome of their plea. How am I to feel? Some have been asked to give their opinion. I have not. Even though I had officially asked the government to keep me informed of developments, they have not done so, despite an official promise that they would.

In 1996 I wrote to the Minister of Justice in South Africa asking for information on developments regarding the case of Richard's murder. Up until that time, all I knew was that some of the perpetrators of the killing had been apprehended, but not all. It was all very vague, at least from my point of view. In due course I received a response from the Head of Ministerial Services, as the Minister of Justice was very busy at the time. He wrote, 'It is difficult to say what has happened in respect of each case.' I would have thought that the Department of Justice would have had a full file on this case given the national, if not international, impact of its implications. But perhaps not. I was, however, directed to the Office of the Attorney-General of the Western Cape, the region in which the crime was committed. It was from here that I was informed: 'They intend to apply to the Truth and Reconciliation Commission for indemnity . . . You will be informed of the outcome of the proceedings.' This letter was dated 21st June 1996.

'You will be informed . . .' Fourteen months after that promise was made, I had still no word on developments and had not even been informed that the hearings had in fact taken place in July 1997.

It was curious that, in a parallel case, the parents of Amy Biehl, a young American exchange student who was killed exactly one month after Richard and whose murderers also applied to the Truth and Reconciliation Commission, were kept informed and flew out from the United States to attend proceedings in South Africa. Mary and I were not afforded the same courtesy. We received only some newspaper cuttings after the event from a friend in Cape Town who thought we might be interested!

It could be argued that I was represented at the hearings by those who spoke on behalf of the Church. However, I was not approached for comment by anyone. My opinion was not sought or asked for from any circle. My family's feelings were not addressed. Plainly, we were *not* represented. It was a statement that said: you are forgotten and we don't care to keep you informed.

Could this happen in Britain? Let us imagine that the man who murdered those little children in Dunblane had not killed himself but stood trial for his crime. Let us also imagine that he then appealed to a special hearing for indemnity because of mitigating circumstances, for that is what the Truth and Reconciliation Commission is all about. Let us take our hypothetical case a step further and say that the parents of the victims were not informed that such a hearing was to take place. Could this happen in Britain? The notion is ludicrous!

But, I can hear some say, are not these the responses of a bereaved and bitter man? No, they are not. As I have said before and shall say again later, I have forgiven the killers their actions, even though none have apologised to me and my family. I simply believe I should have been afforded the courtesy of being kept informed. After all, I was promised that this would be the case.

Richard died protecting his two teenage girlfriends from the gunfire. Their own testimony says that his last thought was for their safety. It is a memorial to courage that few can claim. If he was ever proud of his father, there can be few fathers who are as proud as I am of my son.

And what of the Christian community in Cape Town? What of their response in all this? I can't answer that question. Like me, they too were greatly traumatised. Sadly, I have little contact with them these days. But what of their future?

It is a well-documented fact that the Church often grows

in times of adversity, if not numerically then certainly spiritually. I believe this will be the case in South Africa. But let me be quick to add that adversity may not take the form of overt oppression. I do not foresee Christians being fed to the lions or any such barbaric treatment. The economic and fiscal restraints on South Africa will put far more demands on the followers of Christ and the population in general. Up until the start of the 1990s was a time of plenty for most white people, but the lean years of hardship could well be upon them now. When I was a child I never saw a white person begging in the street; now it is commonplace. When I grew up and sought work, there was never any question that I would find a job – it was guaranteed. Today, affirmative action means that if you are white and middle-class, with no family business to step into, you may well have to seek employment outside the borders of the country. Things like money, jobs and security, that most people took for granted, are simply not readily available any more. It is here that the test of faith will be proved.

Hardship is not always a bad thing. It can be a refining experience as men and women enter stormy waters. The gods of this world are often then shaken from their grasp. For the most part the white man's god had been his gold, dug unwillingly from the ground by the massive black workforce. Now this gold is no longer his. He will have to rely on another God.

How then should we live? Dr Francis Schaeffer asked this penetrating question in his thoughtful and provocative book of the same name. It is a question that can be asked of all South Africans as they hold hands into the millennium.

Lightning Strikes Twice

That the country has lived through a miracle is of little debate. In my studies of history, both ancient and modern, I have never read of a nation with such a potential for bloodshed in the build-up to change, yet so free from it in the actual transition to that change. The reason for it? The grace and mercy of God. There can be no other reason. Just as His hand saved the Ninevites of old from the prophecies and warnings of Jonah, so it held back the forces of evil in South Africa during April 1994. All over the world people in little huddles and in great cathedrals, in home fellowships and crumbling country churches, prayed for restraint. I was greatly moved, in so many places in England, to hear these prayers. And in most cases people did not know that a South African was sitting among them! Make no mistake about it, South Africans owe a great debt to God and His praying people. But how then shall we live?

For my part, should the perpetrators of Richard's murder be set free, they must know that what they did that fateful, wet Sunday night in July 1993 was wicked and evil beyond description. And should they know in their hearts that they have *not* repented of it, then they will one day face another tribunal, one far more severe, far more just and far more penetrating than they have ever known. Then they will have to give an account to the Great Judge before His sentencing, which is final. Then they will stare my son in the face and see what they have wrought. There will be no reconciliation then, only truth. But should they truly repent now, in this life, should they turn to Christ in repentance and faith, then they, like me, will fall into the arms of a merciful God who has bought their blood, and mine, with His own.

Should they be set free, would I seek my own justice?

No, of course not. Vengeance is not mine to take, but God's, and I cannot offer forgiveness on behalf of God. I know that I have forgiven them only on my behalf. I might not have wanted to forgive them, but I have chosen to forgive them. I would, however, grieve that justice in a so-called civilised society had not prevailed. For then I would be in greater fear of the peril that lurks in South Africa than for my own loss. We simply cannot continue to make excuses for base criminality. That is why God has given us the magistrate, to be a terror to evil. The sword and the scales.

Arthur Pink in his excellent comment on the subject says:

> Magistrates and judges were never ordained by God for the purpose of reforming reprobates or pampering degenerates, but to be His instruments for preserving law and order by being a terror to evil. As Romans chapter 13 says, they are to be 'a revenger to execute wrath on him that doeth evil' . . . Conscience has become comatose. The requirements of justice are stifled; maudlin concepts now prevail. As eternal punishment was repudiated – either tacitly or in many cases openly – ecclesiastical punishments are shelved. Churches refuse to endorse sanction and wink at flagrant offences. The inevitable outcome has been the breakdown of discipline in the home and the creation of public opinion which is mawkish and spineless. Schoolteachers are intimidated by foolish parents and children so that the rising generation are more and more allowed to have their own way without the fear of consequences. And if some judge

has the courage of his convictions, and sentences a brute for maiming an old woman, there is an outcry against the judge *(An Exposition of the Sermon on the Mount)*.

If South Africa wants a society that is free from fear, then she must do what is right. That is how she must live. Criminal behaviour must receive criminal justice in the fear of God and the face of the people. For what is the freedom this country sought so long, with so many tears and with so much blood, if it is a freedom of fear? Why, it is no freedom at all. Many people in South Africa today, black and white, coloured and Asian, are living behind fences of sprawling razor wire and electronic gates. They carry firearms and own large dogs. Security companies and armed response organisations are flourishing. Is this how she must live? Is this how her children must grow?

South Africa will have to replant her roots, just as I have had to replant mine. If she does not, and if her people continue on a path apart from civilised law and the restraints of God, then she will plunge into an abyss far blacker than the terrors of the apartheid years.

In April 1994, this beautiful country and its amazing people stepped back from the precipice of disaster. They defied history to repeat itself and raise its bloody fist in violent revolution. There was no bloodbath, but how far back they have stepped from the brink remains to be seen. I fear that it is not far enough. South Africa is winking at crime, embracing modernity which says that all religions are the same and that things will get better. She still allows herself the luxury of blaming the so-called legacy of apartheid' for rising and rampant crime. It is a folly. It is exceedingly unwise, and it is now time to come of age and grow up. I recently watched a BBC television programme with interest, as a well-known white South African author was all too quick to accuse the hurts of the past for the crimes of the present. If that were true, then all aggrieved black people, of which there are many thousands, would be bent on crime. They are not. They are patient still. However, the basic needs of these patient people of South Africa remain unchanged. That is where the real problem lies.

Now the watching world has stopped watching; I scarcely read of any South African events in the international press. And the praying world has ceased to pray. How now can she live?

At the end of the day it is still God's work, His Church, and His will be done. I have no crystal ball into which I can gaze. And even if I had such a thing I would not trust it as much as the One who finally writes all history.

If I have learned one thing over the last five years it is this, that people who fight battles and carry burdens for God's sake are often candidates for blessing. Hardship is no less a thing today than it was in Paul's day. He tells us that God will not desert us even though we may believe that he has. I have seen the hand of God heavy upon me and I have also seen his blessing.

Torn Roots Replanted:
North Devon, 28th August 1997

*Persecuted, but not abandoned; struck down, but
not destroyed.*

(2 Cor. 4:9)

Abbotsham is a tiny village in the heart of North Devon.
It is the sort of village that dreams and movies are made
of. It has a parish church with a Norman tower high on the
hill for all to see and a winding road to the bottom which
leads to a thatched village pub, not surprisingly called the
Thatched Inn. There is a little village store which is also the
post office, a village hall and a village school. Almost every
house and cottage has flower-filled hanging baskets on the
walls and roses of all colours around the doorways.

It is predominantly sheep and dairy farming country,
with a pleasant mix of the old and the new. Patchwork
fields are enclosed by high hedgerows and very narrow
roads. If you should chance to meet an oncoming fellow
motorist it invariably results in someone reversing until
a gap of suitable size in the hedge is reached which
enables both cars to pass. The towns of Bideford and
Barnstaple are close at hand as Abbotsham lies just south
of the Taw–Torridge estuary. With beautiful Exmoor to

the north-east, treacherous and majestic Dartmoor to the south and the rugged North Devon coastline washed by the waters of the Bristol Channel on the north-west, it is one of the principal holiday resorts in Britain. It is quiet here. It is laid back. It is out of the 'fast-lane' and a place where a person can be still with himself and with his Maker.

And it is here that God has put us gently down and allowed the storm clouds to pass.

I mentioned in the previous chapter that our torn roots had been replanted. That is exactly what has happened. In February 1997 we exchanged contracts on a little flower-bedecked cottage and have started over again. In this, we have most certainly seen the providing hand of God. Our meagre capital from South Africa had been eroded by devaluation, but fortunately both Mary and I have found satisfying work in what is one of the most constrained financial regions of the country. Mary is now caring for the aged and enjoys it immensely. Catherine, now nearly eighteen, is into her final year of her A levels and plans to enter university and continue her studies. Amanda, who is now twenty-five, is well into her degree at Canterbury where she studies English and French Law. I have deliberately avoided talking too much about my daughters in this book as it has essentially been about my reaction to the death of their brother. Their reaction has been different. They have stood by and watched their father hurt by ministry, their mother torn by grief, their home pulled from around them, their friends and country left behind and their brother shot by terrorists. They have been hurt by it all, of this there can be little doubt. Like Mary and me, they too had to start again. Their determination and courage is testimony to their character.

I take my boat on the river and along the coast a lot now. It is a rubber inflatable with quite a powerful engine. Richard and I used to have a good deal of fun in it some years ago in the South Atlantic. Now I take other children and listen to their shrieks of delight as we crash over the waves in the North Atlantic. Sometimes I do not take the children. I go on my own and watch the sun sink into the same ocean that now carries my son's ashes – somewhere.

Someone once asked me where I got my strength from. Strength for what? Not crying when people felt I should? Seeming to cope when my mind was filled by memories of a teenage boy, lost? Of what he might have been today and what he could have achieved tomorrow? What is this thing called Christian strength? I never felt I was strong. I never felt in control of the situation. I felt completely crushed and crumpled inside. Sometimes a brave face is a false face, not only a face for a watching world but a face for an expectant Church that wants to see triumph over tragedy. But is there such a thing? Is it often just an illusion, a deceitful mask to hide behind? Christians claim to be triumphant when in reality many are broken and bowed low. Some take years to recover from tragedy, and some never do. The Church expects to hear the claim of forgiveness and recovery from the hurting, and in some cases pressure can be applied by this expectancy. In the case of the massacre in Cape Town there was an instant, wide and shining-eyed response from the Christian community: 'We forgive,' was the almost universal cry. That it had a profound effect on the media was most apparent. In some cases it was an honest response; in many cases it was a stunned expected response, but let me tell you that there

ere times in quiet corners and behind closed doors when
here was quite a different response. It hardly seemed a
'Christian response'. It was not a response for the press,
not a response for the world, but an angry response before
God: 'Why did you let this happen to *me*?' And I was not
the only one making it.

In some circles it has become unacceptable for a believer
to say, 'You've hurt me and I'm bloody angry.' And so,
many believers turn inwards and hold on to their pain. They
say they are 'fine' when in fact they are not. Is this Christian
strength? They fall into despair, but nobody must know.
Is this Christian strength? God doesn't expect this reponse
from us, so why should the Church? Books abound: *Up
From the Fire*, *A Thorn In My Side*, *Smiling Through the
Tears*, *Triumph and Tragedy Can be Bedfellows* – the list
is endless. Few of them expect the Christian to fall on his
pile of ashes and say, with Job, 'May the day of my birth
perish . . . may no shout of joy be heard in it . . . for it
did not shut the doors of the womb on me to hide trouble
from my eyes (Job 3:3, 7, 10). Please remember Job 1:1,
'In the land of Uz there lived a man whose name was Job.
This man was blameless and upright; he feared God and
shunned evil.' A good man, a godly man, who was honest
enough to say, 'I am a man in anguish.' A man who could
cry out in hope from utter despair, 'Though he slay me, yet
will I hope in him' (Job 13:15). A man who did not have a
plethora of Christian 'how to' books to fall back on. All
he did have was his patience, his pain and his God. And
he did not deny any of these their place in his life. His
strength was seen in holding on to the promises of God
even though he was reduced to nothing. And while he sat
there, the world and its wife passed him by.

The only time the Christian Church has seen real triumph is in what the world sees as defeat, a blood-splattered cross and an empty tomb. The only time there will be any real triumph for me in my situation is at the return of Christ. There can be no triumph in Richard's death, only in his resurrection. For I believe in the resurrection of the dead and the life of the world to come. I do. I really do. I have been called a fool and a lot of other things beside because of it, but in that simple statement of faith I find my end and my beginning. Is it not the hope of the Christian? Is it not here that we find our Christian strength?

But for now I have learned contentment. I have not been restored as Job was. I do not have 'fourteen thousand sheep, six thousand camels, a thousand yoke of oxen and a thousand donkeys'. I do not have seven sons, but I do have my wife and my two daughters. I have my health and I have my hope. I also have the promises of God. In *that* I find my Christian strength. Torn roots are back in the soil and the storm is past – for now.

A WITNESS FOR EVER

Michael Cassidy

Michael Cassidy reveals what went on behind the scenes, away from the dramatic headlines, as South Africa inched its way towards the momentous elections of April 1994. A plane with a faulty dial, a prayer meeting with 30,000 people, a Kenyan diplomat, Christian leaders working backstage – all played a part in what newspapers worldwide hailed as a miracle.

Describing the unbearable suspense as the situation teetered on the brink of disaster and the sheer joy when a solution was reached just six days before the elections, Michael Cassidy maintains that, whatever the future holds for South Africa, the extraordinary events leading up to April '94 deserve to be held up as a witness to the power of God.

Michael Cassidy is the founder of African Enterprise and the author of a number of books including *Bursting the Wineskins, The Passing Summer* and *The Politics of Love*

ISBN 0 340 63032 9